ST/ESA/PAD/SER.E/135

Department of Economic and Social Affairs

Reconstructing Public Administration after Conflict:

Challenges, Practices and Lessons Learned

World Public Sector Report 2010

UNITED NATIONS
New York, 2010

DESA Mission Statement

The Department of Economic and Social Affairs of the United Nations Secretariat is a vital interface between global policies in the economic, social and environmental spheres and national action. The Department works in three main interlinked areas: (i) it compiles, generates and analyses a wide range of economic, social and environmental data and information on which Member States of the United Nations draw to review common problems and to take stock of policy options; (ii) it facilitates the negotiations of Member States in many intergovernmental bodies on joint courses of action to address ongoing or emerging global challenges; and (iii) it advises interested Governments on the ways and means of translating policy frameworks developed in United Nations conferences and summits into programmes at the country level and, through technical assistance, helps build national capacities. ◆

Note

The designations employed and the presentation of the material in this publication do not imply the expression of any opinion whatsoever on the part of the Secretariat of the United Nations concerning the legal status of any country, territory, city or area, or of its authorities, or concerning the delimitation of its frontiers or boundaries.

The designations "developed" and "developing" economies are intended for statistical convenience and do not necessarily imply a judgment about the stage reached by a particular country or area in the development process. The term "country" as used in the text of this publication also refers, as appropriate, to territories or areas. The term "dollar" normally refers to the United States dollar ($).

The views expressed are those of the individual authors and do not imply any expression of opinion on the part of the United Nations. ◆

A United Nations Publication

Publication No.: ST/ESA/PAD/SER.E/135

April 2010

UNITED NATIONS

Preface

Since the World Public Sector Report was launched in 2001, it has become a major reference on governance and public administration trends and issues for policymakers, the academia and practitioners from around the world. So far, five editions of this series have been published in a number of crucial thematic areas, including "Globalization and the State", 2001; "E-government at the Crossroads", 2003; "Unlocking the Human Potential for Public Sector Performance", 2005, and "People Matter: Civic Engagement in Public Governance", 2008. In 2008, at its Seventh Session, the United Nations Committee of Experts on Public Administration recommended that the Department of Economic and Social Affairs focus its 2010 World Public Sector Report on "lessons learned in reconstructing governance and public administration after violent conflict".

This 2010 Report brings to the fore a very critical issue - how to reconstruct public administration in post-conflict situations so as to enable it to promote peace and development in countries that have been affected by civil war and destruction. It is a question that has remained unresolved for decades and has brought poverty, despair, and death to people in many corners of the world. Over 20 million people have died since World War II because of civil wars, and many more have been internally displaced*.

This Report shows that no progress can be made in promoting peace, development and protection of human rights unless appropriate governance and public administration institutions are established. Such institutions can help mediate differences and set the foundations for an effective, efficient, transparent, accountable and innovative government. This Report emphasizes that there are no "one size fits all" solutions to governance challenges in post-conflict situations. In each country, public administration reforms should be tailored to local needs.

This Report also highlights that institutions will be meaningful when there are effective leadership and competent civil servants in the public sector. But leaders and civil servants cannot accomplish the mission of re-establishing peace and development on their own. The process of reconstruction can lead to an inclusive and sustainable peace

---

* Collier and Sambanis 2005, p.ix.

only by involving all stakeholders. Finally, unless newly established governments are able to provide essential public services to the population, including safety, security, health, education, shelter, access to water and sanitation and job opportunities, there will be no durable peace. Tensions over access to scarce economic and natural resources will rapidly re-escalate and lead to more violence.

The Report also highlights that contrary to commonly held belief, post-conflict situations not only present challenges, but also numerous opportunities to leapfrog stages of development by adopting innovative practices in public administration, particularly the application of ICTs in government and service delivery. By illustrating some of the most critical issues and strategies for public sector capacity building in countries emerging from conflict, this Report provides an important contribution to a better understanding of the difficulties, but also of the opportunities that countries face in rebuilding their public administration institutions, mechanisms and processes in their quest for durable peace and sustainable development. ◆

SHA Zukang
Under Secretary-General for Economic and Social Affairs

Acknowledgments

The 2010 World Public Sector Report (WPSR) was finalized, under the overall guidance of Jomo Kwame Sundaram, United Nations Assistant Secretary-General for Economic and Social Affairs (DESA), by the Division for Public Administration and Development Management (DPADM). Within the Division, a team of experts lead by Haiyan Qian, Director of DPADM, produced the report. John-Mary Kauzya, Chief of the Governance and Public Administration Branch and Adriana Alberti, Governance and Public Administration Officer in DPADM, coordinated the final production of the publication. Adriana Alberti also authored Chapter I, together with Peride K. Blind, former Governance and Public Administration Officer in DPADM, Chapter II together with John-Mary Kauzya and Chapter III. John-Mary Kauzya is the author of Chapter IV. Chapter V was prepared by Valentina Resta, Governance and Public Administration Officer, DPADM, and Chapter VI was authored by Seema Hafeez, Senior Governance and Public Administration Officer, DPADM. Kathryn Dahl provided external technical editing and copy-editing. This publication was designed by Eliot Sela, a design director consultant. Lois Warner, Associate Governance and Public Administration Officer in DPADM, provided support in finalizing the references. Roseanne Greco provided administrative support, and Mutya Delos Reyes, an intern at DESA, helped format the report.

The WPSR team benefited from the technical advice of in-house colleagues, including Alphonse Mekolo, Atnafu Almaz, Garegin Manukyan, Ulrich Graute, Yoshinobu Yonekawa and Lois Warner, and from the comments of Gay Rosenblum-Kumar and Anita Estroneffer at the Bureau for Crisis Prevention and Recovery in the United Nations Development Programme (UNDP). DESA, through DPADM, has done a great deal of work in the field of governance and public administration, including in countries emerging from conflict. DPADM has engaged in analytical studies, advocacy and capacity-building in post-conflict societies by fostering dialogue and providing government officials with concrete tools to manage conflict. Moreover, to help countries prevent conflict from occurring or recurring, DPADM has increasingly focused on strategies to integrate conflict-sensitive policies and conflict-prevention measures into public administration systems, institutions and practices.

Invaluable input for the report also came from various organizations dealing with issues related to rebuilding governance and public administration. We are grateful to the Center for Global Peace and Conflict Studies at the University of California, Irvine; South Africa's Centre for Conflict Resolution; the German Agency for Technical Cooperation; the International Development Research Centre; the U.K.'s Department for International Development; the United Nations Capital Development Fund; the United Nations Economic Commission for Africa; the United Nations Development Fund for Women; selected UNDP country offices; the UNDP Regional Bureau for Asia and the Pacific; the UNDP Regional Centre for Eastern and Southern Africa; UNDP's Bureau for Policy Development; the United Nations Peace Building Support Office; United Nations Department of Economic and Social Affairs; the University of California, Irvine (USA); the University for Peace; the University of Denver; the World Bank; and the Woodrow Wilson International Center for Scholars. ◆

Executive Summary

The World Public Sector Report is produced by DPADM every two years as a research and analytical tool to provide policymakers and civil society with relevant research findings, information and lessons learned on subjects related to the public sector. It also addresses emerging issues, trends and innovative practices in governance and public administration from around the world, with a particular focus on those that contribute to the realization of the United Nations Development Agenda, including the Millennium Development Goals. The report was established following the recommendations of the Group of Experts on the United Nations Programme on Public Administration and Finance (later renamed the Committee of Experts on Public Administration) at its fifteenth session in 2000. The Economic and Social Council endorsed this recommendation in its resolution E/RES/45/2001.

The main objective of the 2010 World Public Sector Report is to analyse challenges, practices and lessons learned in rebuilding public administration after conflict. The report is intended for decision makers in conflict or conflict-prone situations; personnel in regional and international organizations; practitioners and experts involved in reconstructing governance and public administration, particularly in developing countries and transition economies; educators, scholars and students at academic institutions, think-tanks and policy centres; and interested laypersons. The report is also intended to facilitate and inform discussions of United Nations inter-governmental bodies on issues related to governance and public administration reconstruction in post-conflict situations.

Several reports and studies have been written on how to restore peace after violent conflict, focusing mainly on peacemaking, peacebuilding and economic and social recovery. This report focuses exclusively on rebuilding public administration in post-conflict situations. It is unique in providing key lessons learned about transforming governments to gain trust from citizens and promote peaceful coexistence, sustainable development and prosperity for all.

The report is based on a literature review of the main theories and issues involved in post-conflict reconstruction, coupled with an analysis of relevant case studies and good practices from all five regions of the world, dating from the end of World War II to the present. DPADM also organized three ad hoc expert group meetings—in Mozambique in 2005, in Cameroon in 2006 and in Ghana in 2008—which yielded insightful discussion of technical papers and practical cases. In addition, at United Nations Headquarters in November 2008, a panel of the Second Committee of the General Assembly discussed the topic of State capacity for post-conflict reconstruction. Participants at these events provided invaluable inputs; they included representatives from the Center for Global Peace and Conflict Studies at the University of California, Irvine; South Africa's Centre for Conflict Resolution; the German Agency for Technical Cooperation; the International Development Research Centre; the U.K.'s Department for International Development; the United Nations Capital Development Fund; the United Nations Economic Commission for Africa; the United Nations Development Fund for Women; selected United Nations Development Programme (UNDP) country offices; the UNDP Regional Bureau for Asia and the Pacific; the UNDP Regional Centre for Eastern and Southern Africa; UNDP's Bureau for Policy Development; the United Nations Peace Building Support Office; United Nations Headquarters; the University of California, Irvine; the University for Peace; the University of Denver; the World Bank; and the Woodrow Wilson International Center for Scholars.

The report identifies a number of lessons learned and recommendations for governments in post-conflict situations. They can be summarized as follows.

1. Rebuilding Trust in Government Institutions:
A Key Challenge in Post-Conflict Reconstruction

Countries emerging from conflict situations face a number of unique challenges in rebuilding their public administration systems—ensuring peace and security, fostering social reconciliation and promoting development. Success depends largely on the effectiveness of public administration and the promotion of an efficient, effective, transparent, accountable and innovative government that works in partnership with all stakeholders. The public service is the connecting link between the State and the people, and as such, it is the incubator of public trust or mistrust in government. Other factors may also play a role, but people are most likely to trust government when public servants effectively deliver desired services in a timely manner, behave transparently and ethically, demonstrate accountability and integrity, are responsive to the needs of the people and mirror the diversity within the population.

In each country, depending on the past and present government institutions, structures, practices and leadership capacities, the needs for reconstruction vary greatly. In Rwanda, for example, after the 1994 genocide, the public administration system was completely destroyed and could not be reformed; it had to be rebuilt. Similarly, in Timor-Leste and in Kosovo, the United Nations had to intervene to re-establish public administration. In other cases, however, where relatively strong institutions existed before the outbreak of violence, reform and reconfiguration would be most appropriate. A common denominator, however, is that the public service must be seen to be fundamentally and positively different from the previous government. This is often a challenge, if the public administration that is supposed to enact reforms is the same one that contributed, either directly or indirectly, to the original conflict. In order to rebuild trust, appropriate institutions, systems and mechanisms need to be put in place to engage citizens in identifying their needs and priorities, as well as in planning, implementing and evaluating policies, programmes and public services that are citizen-centric and equitable.

2. **Effective Leadership:**
The Key Ingredient in Post-conflict Reconstruction

The root causes of intrastate conflict are usually assumed to be poverty and economic inequality or clashes among different ethnic or religious groups. However, the central cause of violent conflict is weak governance institutions characterized by a lack of predictable and sustainable systems and by leaders who use public office to benefit themselves and their affiliates. The result is divisive politics based on the monopolization of power and the exclusion of major social and political groups. Factional disputes and the State's inability to function effectively, let alone achieve economic and social progress, breed violent conflict. In Uganda, for example, rebel groups took up arms in response to a succession of autocratic leaders who repressed the opposition and were accused of rigging the 1980 general elections. In Rwanda, a succession of Hutu-dominated governments excluded and expelled Tutsis, triggering a Tutsi-led armed rebellion that in turn led the Hutus to try exterminating the Tutsi in the 1994 genocide. In Somalia, Siad Barre monopolized power from 1969 until 1991 by favoring his own clan and imprisoning and killing opponents. Therefore, a major priority of post-conflict governance is to transform previous patterns of divisive oppositional politics.

Developing leadership capacities in post-conflict countries is pre-eminently an endogenous process that can be aided by impartial facilitators and by donor-supported initiatives to bring contending parties together and to strengthen the capacities of the capacity builders. Leadership is critical in post-conflict situations to establish appropriate systems and institutions, to enhance human resources, to judiciously manage scarce resources, to promote knowledge and last but not least, to promote innovation and technological usage. Leaders must have a vision of the future in order to implement institutional reforms. They must also be able to mobilize the people around them to move reforms in the right direction and achieve shared goals.

It is not possible to transform public administration without transforming the beliefs, attitudes and behaviours of leaders and civil servants so that they perform effectively within a democratic setting. Thus, although there is a great emphasis on building technical and managerial skills, it is equally important to develop trust between leaders of competing factions and among competing factions themselves. Most importantly, the perception of politics as a zero-sum game needs to be transformed into a mindset that emphasizes collaboration and respect for the underlying values and principles of agreed-upon governance institutions. Leadership and institutional development are symbiotic. Leaders create institutions, but they must then be willing to accept to submit themselves to those institutions. Unless a political and technical leadership emerges after conflict to champion the creation and operationalization of the right institutions, no lasting peace can be guaranteed.

3. **Appropriate Institution-Building:**
Establishing Formal Rules of Governance Is Not Enough;
Their Underlying Values and Belief Systems Must Also Be
Internalized by All Actors

Rebuilding appropriate governance and public administration institutions, systems and mechanisms is undoubtedly one of the most critical issues in ensuring peace and security, human rights and socio-economic development in countries emerging from violent conflict. Every post-conflict situation is unique and requires a unique institutional development strategy, which should begin from an accurate assessment of the past. The degree of institutional development needed in each country depends on the nature of the systems and institutions, practices and behaviours, and local political culture that were present before the upsurge of violence. Redesigning democratic institutions in countries where they previously existed is very different from designing new governance institutions where there were none before. In addition, institution-building is affected by the duration of a conflict and the way it ends (whether with a negotiated peace settlement, a power-sharing arrangement, or the outright victory of one party).

One of the most challenging yet vital tasks for a country in the aftermath of civil war is to create a common vision for the future. Aspirations for socio-politico-economic development—and the challenges that stand in the way—should be discussed and agreed in consultation with a cross-section of the population. At the same time, discussions must address how responsibilities will be shared among different stakeholders and what mechanisms will be used to encourage collaboration and participation by all sectors (public, private and civil society). In South Africa, for example, the African National Congress leadership prepared a White Paper outlining its proposals for transforming the public service, and then invited—and received—extensive public comment. The White Paper proved to be a very effective mechanism for ensuring public participation and achieving unity in the country.

The main challenge is not designing new institutions per se, but promoting mechanisms to ensure that public servants behave according to agreed-upon rules and values. In other words, the formal rules and the underlying values and belief systems must be well understood, shared and internalized by all stakeholders.

Because post-conflict situations are heterogeneous, there are no "one size fits all" institutional solutions to governance challenges. In each country, institutional reforms should be tailored to current needs while taking into account the legacy of pre-existing institutions, including past values and belief systems. Rebuilding the same institutions that led to violent conflict should be avoided, but some traditional practices might be worthy of retaining or creatively adapting. Uganda, for example, reintroduced kingdoms and traditional leadership institutions but conferred on them missions related to economic development and cultural development. Rwanda introduced the gacaca court system, based on traditional communal law-enforcement practices, to meet the challenges brought about by the genocide of 1994.

Effective institution-building rests on the following steps: (i) designing, through dialogue with stakeholders, a comprehensive national programme for strengthening governance and public administration; (ii) developing a shared vision and clear mission for governance and public administration institutions; (iii) enshrining the principles of good governance in formal frameworks such as written constitutions; (iv) harmonizing traditional and modern institutions; (e) promoting participatory democracy and local governance; and (f) building an infrastructure for peace, including institutions and mechanisms to mediate disputes.

4. **A Capable and Inclusive Pubic Service:**
A Central Actor in the Reconstruction Process

The public service is integral to the social, political, economic and cultural life of every country. Consequently, in conflict situations, the public service is generally both a contributing factor to the conflict and a casualty of it. It is also a central actor in the reconstruction process, and as such, the public service must transform itself so that it can appropriately manage the changed and changing public administration environment.

The success of government in a post-conflict society depends on the performance of the public service in providing critical services to the population and restoring trust and confidence in governance. Public servants are engaged in every facet of government activity—education, health care, public safety, infrastructure, environmental protection, etc.,—and most of them work directly with citizens, to whom they represent the face of government. Therefore, the quality of public servants in terms of knowledge, skills, ethics, attitudes and networks can make or break public trust in a post-conflict government. This makes capacity-building in the public service essential for post-conflict recovery.

The human resources challenges that countries face after conflict are serious, since many skilled government workers die or flee to other countries. Timor-Leste, for example, lost an estimated 7,000 civil servants after Indonesian rule collapsed in 1999, leaving a vacuum in all areas of government. Uganda had a very different problem after its civil war ended in 1986. Uganda's post-conflict public service was overstaffed—bloated by redundant positions with overlapping functions. Ghost workers on the State payroll also create problems. Countries in such situations may find that they do not have enough staff to run the public service, yet payroll records reveal more employees than the budget can support.

Another challenge in reconstructing human resources in the public service after conflict is modifying the behaviour of public servants. In all cases, violence not only thins the ranks of the civil service, but also warps the behaviour and motivation of those who remain. In Bosnia and Herzegovina, for example, the war was the beginning of totally unacceptable practices in the public sector. The political parties in power protected certain ethnic and religious interests, and corruption and nepotism flourished. Uganda's public service was likewise plagued by corrupt or uncommitted personnel.

In most post-conflict and crisis situations, there are also tensions among various ethnic, socio-politico-cultural or religious groups. Such situations are ripe for conflict and need to be carefully managed. South Africa, for example, by emphasizing reconciliation and inclusiveness, successfully managed to turn its diversity to an advantage and create a pluralistic workforce of high-performing public servants.

Reconstruction efforts should proceed from an accurate count of a country's public servants and an accurate picture of their knowledge and skills. Because employee censuses are expensive, they should be planned to fit within the overall strategy for developing human resources in the public service. It is highly desirable for oversight of the recruitment process to be managed by independent bodies such as civil service commissions to avoid cronyism, nepotism, and other forms of favoritism. But because it takes time to create and develop such institutions, interim measures should be devised to address the immediate challenge of recruiting competent personnel. If merit-based recruitment is introduced early, there is a greater chance of limiting patronage and other harmful practices and instead ensuring a well-functioning public service. Efforts must also be made to restore integrity, ethics and professional conduct in the public service. Moreover, diversity within the population should be reflected within the public service. If men and women, as well as members of all ethnic, religious and other groups, are actively included in the government, then conflict is less likely to erupt. A representative, merit-based, service-oriented public service can provide a model for participation, inclusive decision-making, reconciliation and social cohesion, and proactive peacebuilding.

5. Engaging Citizens in Post-Conflict Reconstruction:
An Essential Ingredient for Sustainable Peace

Participatory governance can be fostered in many ways. One key strategy is decentralization, which allows for the shared exercise of power and facilitates the involvement of local communities in policy decisions about their own development. Decentralization is not a panacea, however. If implemented without proper planning and accountability mechanisms, decentralization can reallocate power and resources in a way that leads to power struggles and renewed conflict. Moreover, if it does not empower citizens to participate in decision-making processes so as to ensure that policies are citizen-centric, responsive and sustainable, then decentralization is not effective. How the process is managed has a great impact on its effectiveness as a tool for participation. The engagement of stakeholders in inter-group negotiations reduces the propensity for conflict and fosters social, political and economic stability.

Guatemala's experience is informative because of the extraordinary degree to which decentralization opened doors for civil society—particularly long-marginalized indigenous populations—to take part in the decision making processes of government. Peace accords were signed in Guatemala in 1999 at the end of 36 years of conflict and authoritarian rule. As part of the peace agreement, the Government agreed to reform the municipal code to ensure local input into local decisions through the *cabildo abierto*—the Guatemalan equivalent of the town meeting. The Government also committed to restoring local development councils to ensure that community groups—associations of indigenous people, campesino organizations, women's groups, etc.—help formulate local investment priorities. Guatemala needs to do more to institutionalize the participatory mechanisms it has created, but the emphasis on citizen engagement has helped prevent or resolve some conflicts and laid the foundations for a more peaceful society.

Another positive example is that of South Africa. In 1994, in response to popular demand, the country's first democratically elected Government initiated a post-conflict recovery process that included extensive negotiations for decentralization as well as for a post-apartheid national constitution. The negotiations were crucial for mobilizing all South Africans to accept the principle of empowering local communities and dismantling the apartheid system that had left the country with racially divided business and residential areas. The structural arrangement that facilitated the formulation of these plans was the Integrated Development Plan Representative Forum. It also ensured proper communication between all stakeholders and the municipality, as well as the monitoring of planning and implementation processes. Community members felt empowered to participate and influence the social, political and economic decisions of concern to them.

In Rwanda, the push to decentralize came from the top. After the genocidal conflict in 1994, the government undertook decentralization as part of peacebuilding. Old politico-administrative structures, leadership groups and mentalities were replaced by new ones more suited to promoting peace and social reconciliation. Participatory decision-making, based on local leadership, was encouraged through the establishment of Community Development Committees attended by all community members of voting age. Gender issues were also mainstreamed into development planning, and it was mandated that women should represent 33 per cent of local government council representatives. Although political will was responsible for initiating the decentralization, civic will was cultivated through extensive consultation and sensitization.

Rwanda's efforts to engage women in governance are notable because in many countries, women have been excluded from the negotiating tables and left out of the ensuing peacebuilding processes, despite their vital contributions during the conflict and recovery periods. In Mozambique, to cite just one example, women played a critical role during the liberation struggle that brought independence to the country, but they were totally absent from the Rome peace process that ended the civil war. Arguably, peace cannot be lasting unless both men and women can participate in peacebuilding, influence reconstruction and development efforts and equally enjoy their benefits. Ethnic and religious minorities and other marginalized groups must also be drawn into public administration reconstruction.

Governments in post-conflict settings should adopt strategies aimed at promoting institutionalized collaboration of State and non-State actors in identifying, analyzing and addressing the root causes of conflict. Experiences from around the world clearly point to the critical importance of engaging civil society, in all its diversity, to ensure that actions are responsive to the actual needs of the population. This can be of enormous help in achieving governmental and societal transformation after conflict and bringing countries forward on a path of long-lasting peace and development.

6. Citizen-Centric Service Delivery in Post-Conflict Situations:

The Raison d'Être of Public Administration

Post-Conflict Reconstruction

The fundamental raison d'être of government is the delivery of services to its people. Tragically, in times of violent conflict, attention and resources shift from production to destruction, and the government's capacity to provide services becomes severely impaired. The effects on the population are devastating. In Bosnia and Herzegovina, for example, fewer than 35 per cent of children were immunized during the fighting in 1994, compared with 95 per cent before hostilities broke out. During Liberia's 15-year civil war, at least 50 per cent of all schools were destroyed, depriving 800,000 children of education.

The government's inability to provide security, health care, education, access to clean water and other basic services not only threatens people's welfare; it also erodes the State's credibility and legitimacy. Consequently, restoring effective delivery of public services after violent conflict is necessary not just to ensure the survival of the people, but also to re-establish public trust in government. Improving service delivery can also reduce tensions and grievances among groups struggling to meet basic needs and competing for scarce resources. In this way, strengthening government capacity to provide services becomes a means of promoting peace and spearheading economic development.

In the aftermath of conflict, States rarely have adequate financial, human and other resources to undertake effective reconstruction and rebuilding efforts. In this context, the involvement of multiple stakeholders is necessary. Public officials should adopt an inclusive approach that brings together both State and non-State players, including multilateral and bilateral donors and local and international non-governmental organizations, to solidify public service delivery capacities. However, when foreign donors are involved, there must be an understanding that they are partners in the process, not directors of it. Reconstruction and reform programmes must be designed, decided and implemented with the participation and ownership of nationals. Service delivery systems should be crafted to use local resources, deliver tangible outputs based on need and target the poorest and most marginalized groups. Aid donors took such an approach in Nepal after insurgents declared a "people's war" in 1996. The biggest need for public services was in remote, rural communities, where security concerns made access even more challenging. To successfully provide public services, donors made arrangements on a case by case basis with local community organizations and other partners.

In devising effective strategies for public service delivery, it is important to allow room for flexibility and innovation. Stakeholders also need to recognize the benefits of using information and communications technologies (ICTs) as an integral part of the overall reconstruction of public administration and service delivery capacities in post conflict situations. Information dissemination should be treated as a basic service in post-conflict societies. In the short term, information about security, emergency relief and services for displaced persons and refugees may literally mean the difference between life and death. In the long run, information on various development initiatives, such as public health and education programmes, can contribute to effective service delivery, nation building and sustainable development.

The ICT tools available for communicating information include radio, television, mobile phones and the Internet. For example, during the conflict in the Democratic Repulic of Congo, the United Nations and other donors set up Radio Okapi to help keep peace by disseminating reliable and credible information from an independent source. The free flow of information can also empower public institutions, societal groups and citizens to produce and share knowledge—between and within service delivery sectors—to bring a greater degree of cohesion, transparency and accountability.

New technologies can, moreover, be used to directly facilitate the delivery of more tangible public services. An example is the Sahana disaster management system developed after the Asian tsunami in December 2004. Sahana is an open-source, Web-based collaboration tool that has facilitated the coordination and distribution of relief after natural disasters. Another example is the introduction of new technologies to support the provision of water and electricity at the headquarters of the United Nations Interim Force in Lebanon. The ICTs used there allow for constant monitoring of the water supply levels and the electrical grid. The system enables quick repair of any fault before any operations are affected, minimizing service disruptions and engendering cost savings.

ICTs have not yet been widely incorporated into strategies for improving public service delivery in post-conflict situations. However, the donor community does have considerable experience using ICTs in disaster relief efforts. Various international organizations, non-governmental organizations and private companies have gone beyond the basic applications of ICTs and are providing interactive tools, searchable databases, maps and GIS and electronic forums for disaster management. If such strategies are adapted for use in post-conflict situations, they can transform the whole operation of government, which will enable it to provide citizen-centric, more efficient, effective, transparent, and accountable public services. ◆

Figure 1 **The virtuous cycle of public administration post-conflict reconstruction**

Effective Leadership
Transforming mindsets and promoting beliefs, attitudes and skills that build collaboration is key

A Capable and Inclusive Public Service
A central actor in the reconstruction process

Citizen-Centric and Innovative Public Service Delivery
The raison d'Être of public administration post-conflict reconstruction

The key ingredients for rebuilding public administration after conflict

Appropriate Institution-Building
Establishing formal rules of governance is not enough; their underlying values and belief systems must also be internalized by all actors

Citizens' Engagement
An essential ingredient for sustainable peace

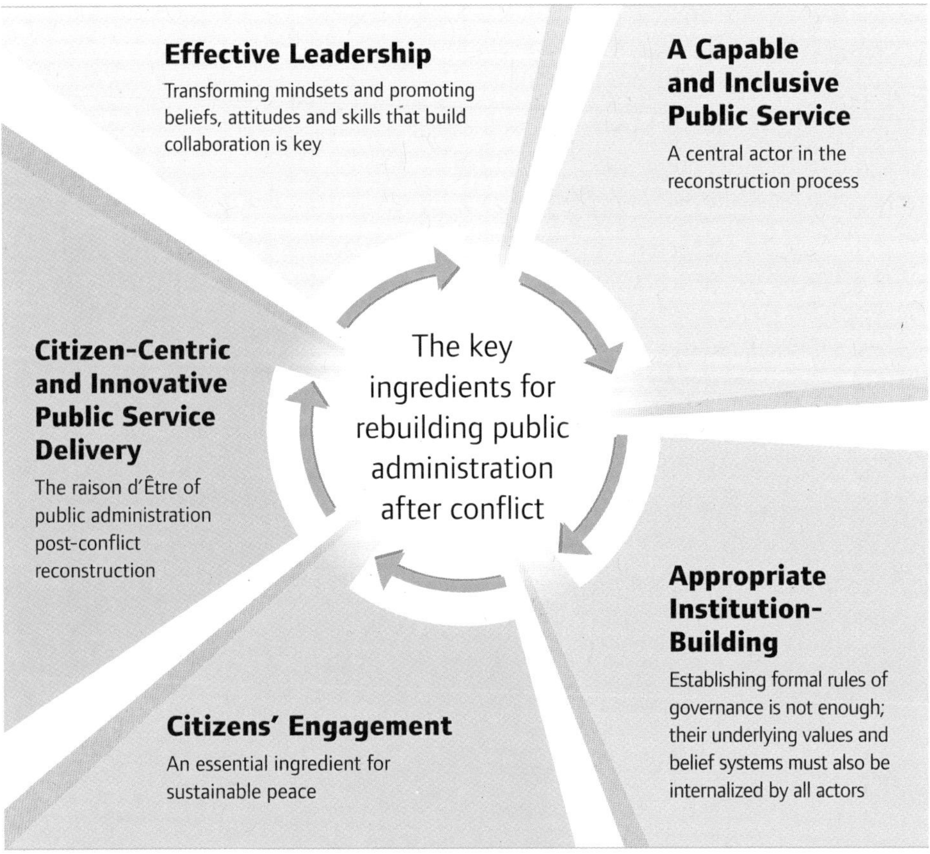

Introduction

This Report is divided into six chapters each one dealing with specific areas of public administration reconstruction after conflict. Moreover, each chapter highlights challenges, strategies, and lessons learned so as to provide concrete policy options. Chapter I analyzes the critical challenges and goals of reconstructing public administration after conflict. It begins by "providing an overview of instrastate violent conflict after World War II. It then attempts to define post-conflict reconstruction" —a relatively new term that is not universally understood. The chapter then presents the overarching goals of post-conflict governments and the specific challenges they face in rebuilding public administration.

Chapter II focuses on leadership capacity-building in post-conflict situations. One of the most critical elements for the success of post-conflict reconstruction is the presence of capable leaders, at all levels of government, who are committed to transforming conflict into peaceful coexistence and collaboration. Yet as energy is exerted on peace negotiations, peacekeeping operations and basic humanitarian assistance, too little attention is paid to cultivating effective leaders and promoting respect for institutions. Instead, the conversation is dominated by discussion about how parties to the conflict should share power and wealth. This approach often reignites conflict, demonstrating the need to focus more sharply on leadership transformation and capacity-building. This chapter looks at the challenges in building effective leadership, the capacities needed by post-conflict leaders and strategies for developing those capacities. The chapter also analyzes the role of international and regional donors in promoting leadership capacity development.

Chapter III looks at institution-building. Institutions are generally defined as the rules of the game in economic, political and social interactions. Put another way, they equate to the formal (e.g., the constitution and party systems) rules and procedures governing human behavior. In governance, institutions encompass (i) all standard operating procedures of governments, (ii) more overarching structures of State, and (iii) a nation's normative social order (Ikenberry 1988). Only recently has attention been given to public administration reforms, including civil service reforms, in post-conflict States. International organizations and donors have often focused on elections as the political tool for institution-building and on macroeconomic development as the economic engine of growth. International financial institutions have prescribed the reduction of public sector expenditures, including civil service expenditures (Vandermoortele 2003). Yet it is equally important, if not more so, to pay explicit attention to institution-building as an ongoing process in post-conflict societies. This chapter begins by looking at the key issues involved in building institutions after conflict. It then discusses ways to strengthen public sector institutions, focusing on the civil service, legislative institutions and the judiciary. It also addresses mechanisms to improve the public sector's performance in delivering public services and preventing relapses into conflict.

Chapter IV explores the critical issue of human resources capacity building in post-conflict situations. The public service is integral to the social, political, economic and cultural life of every country. Consequently, in conflict situations, the public service is generally both a contributing factor to the conflict and a casualty of it. It is also a central actor in the reconstruction process, and as such, the public service must transform itself so that it can appropriately manage the changed and changing public administration environment. This chapter looks first at why a strong public service is so important in post-conflict situations, and how human resources capacity varies from country to country. The chapter then focuses on challenges and strategies related to the development of human resources capacity after conflict. It addresses the following issues: controlling the number of public servants on the payroll; practicing merit-based recruitment; promoting transparency, accountability, integrity, professionalism and ethics; respecting diversity in the public service and tapping its potential benefits; paying civil servants in a post-conflict situation; and counteracting brain drain.

Post-conflict reconstruction is most successful when all segments of society are engaged in the process. Therefore, as part of their efforts to rebuild robust public administration systems, post-conflict countries must seek to involve citizens in decisionmaking. One key strategy in this regard is decentralization—the transfer of powers, functions, responsibilities and resources from the central government to local authorities or other subnational entities. In practical terms, decentralization involves striking a balance between the claims of the periphery and the demands of the centre. Chapter V, therefore, examines decentralization as a mechanism for institutionalizing engaged governance and promoting sustainable peace. It analyzes the concept of decentralization, the challenges in implementing it, and the experiences of several post-conflict countries. The chapter then discusses the importance of engaging two particular constituencies—women and minority groups—in governance, highlighting challenges as well as strategies for success.

The fundamental raison d'être of government is the delivery of services to its people. These include social services (primary education and basic health services), infrastructure (water and sanitation, roads and bridges) and services that promote personal security (justice system and police services), whether provided directly by the public sector or by government-financed private providers. Thus, Chapter VI looks at the challenges and strategies involved in rebuilding capacities for public service delivery. In particular, the chapter analyses the benefits of a multistakeholder approach and the crucial role that information and communication technologies (ICTs) can play. ■

Contents

Abbreviations and Acronyms

ANC African National Congress

APC All Peoples' Congress

BCPR-UNDP Bureau for Conflict Prevention and Recovery

CDCs Community Development Committees

CIAA Commission for Investigation of Abuse of Authority

DAC Development Assistance Committee

DFID United Kingdom Department for International Development

DPADM Division for Public Administration and Development Management

ECA United Nations Economic Commission for Africa

ECOSOC Economic and Social Council

EU European Union

FYROM Former Yugoslav Republic of Macedonia

GDP Gross Domestic Product

GIS Geographic Information Systems

GTZ German Agency for Technical Cooperation

HIIK Heidelberger Institute for International Conflict Research

HIV/AIDS Human Immuno-deficiency Virus/ Acquired Immunodeficiency Syndrome

HRD/M Human Resource Development/ Management

ICT Information and Communications Technology

IDRC International Development Research Centre

IOM International Organization for Migration

IRIN Integrated Regional Integration Network

ITU International Telecommunications Unit

LANS Local Area Network

LDCs Least Developed Countries

LICUS Low Income Countries under Stress

MDGs Millennium Development Goals

NATO North Atlantic Treaty Organization

NGOs Non Governmental Organizations

OCHA United Nations Office for the Coordination Humanitarian Affairs

OECD Organization Economic Cooperation and Development

PACTEC Partners in Technology International

SIGMA Support for Improvement in Governance and Management

TOKTEN Transfer of Knowledge through Expatriate Nationals

TSF Télécoms sans Frontières

UNCDF United Nations Capital Development Fund

UNDESA United Nations Department of Economic and Social Affairs

UNDP United Nations Development Programme

UNHCR United Nations Human Rights Commission

UNIFEM United Nations Development Fund for Women

UNPBC United Nations Peacebuilding Commission

UNPBSO United Nations Peacebuilding Support Office

WANS Wide Area Network

WFP United Nations World Food Program

WHO World Health Organization

WPSR World Public Sector Report

WSIS World Summit for Information Society

Chapter I

Public Administration Challenges after Conflict

This chapter analyzes the critical challenges of reconstructing public administration after conflict. It begins by providing an overview of instrastate violent conflict after World War II. It then attempts to define "post-conflict reconstruction"—a relatively new term that is not universally understood. The chapter then presents the overarching goals of post-conflict governments and the specific challenges they face in rebuilding public administration.

1. Overview of Instrastate Violent Conflict after World War II

Since the end of the Second World War, most armed conflicts have been within states rather than between them—a shift from the inter-state warfare that marked much of the nineteenth and early twentieth centuries. Civil wars around the world "have killed since 1945 approximately 20 million people and displaced at least 67 million"[1]. Civilian deaths as a percentage of all war-related deaths increased from 50 per cent in the eighteenth century to 90 per cent in 1990.

Since 1945 about 20 million people have died and 67 million were displaced due to civil wars

The United Nations High Commissioner for Refugees estimated that in December 2006, there was a global population of 8.8 million registered refugees and as many as 24.5 million internally displaced people in more than 50 countries. The actual global population of refugees is probably closer to 10 million, given the estimated 1.5 million Iraqi refugees displaced throughout the Middle East. Internal wars have not only caused alarmingly high rates of casualties, but they have also contributed to the destabilization of entire regions while causing economic deterioration and exacerbating social inequalities. Moreover, research has shown that of all countries emerging from war, nearly 50 per cent face relapse into conflict within a decade.

Since 1948, the United Nations Security Council has authorized 63 UN peacekeeping operations (see the annex to this report). Just 18 of these were established between 1948 and 1990; 45 operations were established between 1990 and 2008; and 16 are still ongoing. As of late 2009, about 35 countries could be described as having entered a post-conflict phase since the Cold War era (UNDP 2008).

The UN Security Council has authorized 63 UN Peacekeeping operations

The worst intrastate conflicts over the past decades have taken place in the developing world and in newly independent states, particularly in Sub-Saharan Africa (the site of more than 20 civil wars since 1945), the Middle East and Maghreb, Asia and the Pacific, and to a lesser extent, the Americas.[2] In Europe, internal conflicts have erupted in Cyprus, Georgia, Greece, Russia, Spain, the United King-

The worst intrastate conflicts over the past decades have taken place in the developing world

[1] (Collier and Sambanis 2005, p. ix)

[2] Sub-Saharan African countries affected by conflict include Angola, Burundi, Central African Republic, Chad, the Republic of Congo, Djibouti, Ethiopia, Guinea-Bissau, Kenya, Liberia, Mali, Mozambique, Namibia, Nigeria, Rwanda, Senegal, Sierra Leone, Somalia, South Africa, Sudan, Uganda, Zaire/Democratic Republic of Congo and Zimbabwe. In the Middle East and Maghreb, conflict has erupted in Algeria, Egypt, Israel, Lebanon, Morocco/Western Sahara, Jordan and Syria. In Asia and the Pacific, internal conflicts have taken place in Afghanistan, Azerbaijan, Bangladesh, Cambodia, China, India, Indonesia, Iran, Iraq, Laos, Myanmar/Burma, Nepal, Oman, Pakistan, Papua New Guinea, the Philippines, Sri Lanka, Tajikistan, Thailand, Turkey, Vietnam and Yemen. In the Americas, conflicts have erupted in Argentina, Bolivia, Colombia, Costa Rica, Cuba, the Dominican Republic, El Salvador, Guatemala, Haiti, Nicaragua, Paraguay and Peru.

Figure I.1 **Violent conflicts of high intensity in 2007**

War
Severe crises
All other countries

The countries addicted by conflicts are marked regarding the highest intensity

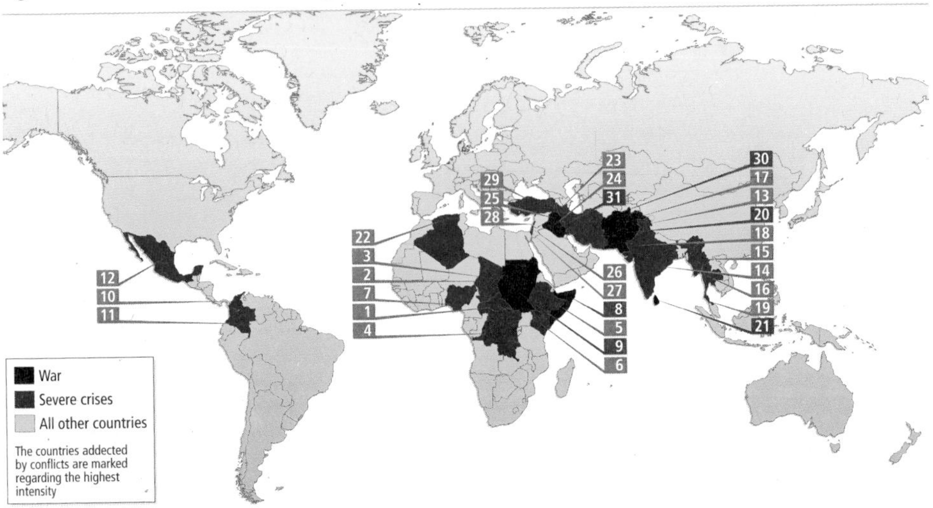

A severe crisis is defined as a conflict involving the repeated use of violent force in an organized way. A war is a conflict in which violent force is used with continuity in an organized and systematic way that results in massive destruction of long duration.

Legend
No. Name and conflict items

Sub-Saharan Africa: Severe crises
1. **Central African Republic** (UFDR, APRD): national power
2. **Chad** (ethnic groups): regional predominance
3. **Chad** (various rebel groups): national power
4. **DR Congo** (ex-RCD-G, Interahamwe, FDLR): national power
5. **Ethiopia** (ONLF/Ogaden): secession
6. **Kenya** (ethnic groups): resources
7. **Nigeria** (Niger Delta/Ijaw): regional predominance, resources

Sub-Saharan Africa: Wars
8. **Somalia** (UIC): system/ideology, national power
9. **Sudan** (Darfur): regional predominance, resources

The Americas: Severe crises
10. **Colombia** (FARC/ELN): system/ideology, regional predominance, resources
11. **Colombia** (FARC): system/ideology, regional predominance,resources
12. **Mexico** (drug cartels) – regional predominance

Asia and Oceania: Severe crises
13. **India** (Kashmir): secession
14. **India** (Naxalites): system/ideology
15. **Myanmar** (KNU, KNLA, KNPP, KnA-UWSA, DKBA, government/Karen State, Kayah State): secession
16. **Myanmar** (opposition): system/ideology, national power
17. **Pakistan** (Islamists): system/ideology
18. **Pakistan** (Sunnites/Shiites): system/ideology, regional predominance
19. **Thailand** (Muslim separatists/southern border provinces): secession

Asia and Oceania: Wars
20. **Pakistan** (North and South Waziristan): regional predominance
21. **Sri Lanka** (LTTE): secession

The Middle East and Maghreb: Severe crises
22. **Algeria** (Islamist groups): system/ideology, national power
23. **Iran** (PJAK/Kurdish areas): autonomy
24. **Iraq** (al-Sadr group): system/ideology, national power
25. **Iraq** (al-Zarqawi group): system/ideology, national power
26. **Israel** (al-Fatah, Hamas): system/ideology, regional predominance
27. **Israel** (PNA, al-Fatah, Hamas/Palestine): secession, system/ideology, resources
28. **Lebanon** (Hezbollah, Fatah al-Islam): system/ideology, national power
29. **Turkey** (PKK/KONGRA-GEL/Kurdish areas): autonomy

The Middle East and Maghreb: Wars
30. **Afghanistan** (Taliban): system/ideology, national power
31. **Iraq** (insurgents): system/ideology, national power

Source: HIIK (2007), p. 2

dom (Ireland) and the former Yugoslavia, including Croatia, Bosnia-Herzegovina and Kosovo. Figure 1 shows violent conflicts of high intensity in 2007.

Since 1945, there have been two major periods in international politics that have directly or indirectly influenced the burgeoning of conflict within countries around the world. First, the end of World War II led to a wave of decolonization and the consequent advent of the international bipolar system and a number of proxy wars. Second, the demise of the Cold War in the early 1990s fed a struggle for independence and self-determination in several nations that were formerly part of the Soviet Union.

During the first historical period—that is, in the aftermath of the Second World War—two different trends in reconstruction and recovery unfolded. Countries in the West received an enormous boost in financial aid and state-building support from a single donor, the United States, through the European Recovery Plan, best known as the Marshall Plan. Meanwhile, countries in other regions of the world were still struggling for political independence. The decolonization movement that occurred between 1946 and 1960 was characterized by peaceful liberation in some countries, and by internal conflict and struggle in others. The high hopes that countries had after gaining independence were often followed by bitter disappointment, as domination by a foreign country was replaced by coups d'états or loss of state authority and political legitimacy. These developments brought an increased use of violent means in order to ensure survival, security and access to resources.

Many of these violent conflicts were exacerbated by the Cold War ideological struggle. The two superpowers did not intend to fight wars directly (because both sides possessed atomic weapons), but they supported a number of proxy wars throughout the world. For example, the Soviet Union encouraged uprisings in Vietnam, Nicaragua, Congo and Sudan as part of its ideological battle against colonization, which it viewed as the epitome of capitalism and imperialism. The United States, for its part, aided factions fighting against the communist ideology. This indirect competition between the superpowers worsened the internal conflicts in several countries by adding more fuel to escalating tensions.

Many of the violent conflicts that erupted after decolonization were exacerbated by the Cold War ideological struggle

Following the end of the Cold War in the early 1990s, a movement for independence and self-determination swept through Eastern Europe. With the dismantling of old state institutions and the complexity of the geo-political and ethnic configuration of nations in the former Eastern Bloc, a number of conflicts erupted within the boundaries of this region. The Western Balkans, for example, suffered increased ethnic and religious strife. Conflicts also developed in countries like Algeria and Afghanistan, as religious fundamentalist groups tried to control political institutions and dominate public life.

With the increase of intrastate wars, international and regional organizations shifted their focus towards issues of peace and security within states rather than between them

As intrastate wars became increasingly common, international and regional organizations such as the United Nations, the North Atlantic Treaty Organization (NATO) and the European Union[3] shifted their focus towards issues of peace and security *within* states rather than between them. State-building—international intervention to restore order and strengthen government institutions in the aftermath of conflict—emerged as a key strategy. This focus is especially needed in the post-9/11 era; there is now heightened awareness that weak states—those that lack the capacity to control their own territory and to implement public policies—can become safe havens for terrorists, drug traffickers and extremist groups. As such, they pose a grave threat to regional and international security.

To help counter this threat and to support peace efforts in countries emerging from conflict, the United Nations Peacebuilding Commission was established in 2005. The Commission now plays a key role in advancing the international community's broad peace agenda. ◆

2. Definition and phases of post-conflict reconstruction

Defining post-conflict reconstruction

In recent years, the concept of "post-conflict reconstruction" has received much attention from scholars and practitioners, as well as from international organizations including the United Nations. Nevertheless, because of the complexities inherent to post-conflict situations, the term continues to lack a precise definition.

The UN started focusing on "post-conflict reconstruction" in the 1990s

Conflict is age-old in the history of humanity, but post-conflict reconstruction has only recently become a domain of international interest (see table I.1). It was not until the 1990s that the United Nations began to focus on post-conflict reconstruction as a distinctive activity, separate from peacemaking, peacekeeping and conflict prevention. In fact, an analysis of United Nations documents written

---

[3] The European Union, originally called the European Community, was created after World War II with the overriding aim of preventing future wars among sovereign states.

Table I.1 **Early use of "post-conflict" terminology by international organizations**

Year	Term	Context
1992	Post-conflict peacebuilding	Post-conflict peacebuilding is highlighted in *An Agenda for Peace*, a United Nations Secretary-General Report.
1995	Post-conflict countries	The International Monetary Fund introduces a new financing instrument for post-conflict countries focusing on institution-building.
1997	Post-conflict reconstruction	The World Bank develops its *Framework for World Bank Involvement in Post-Conflict Reconstruction* and establishes the Post-Conflict Fund. The Organisation for Economic Co-operation and Development establishes the Development Assistance Committee (DAC) and the DAC Task Force to guide investments in post-conflict countries. It also sets up a Conflict Prevention and Conflict Reconstruction Network.
2005	Post-conflict peacebuilding and recovery	The United Nations establishes the Peacebuilding Commission (PBC).

before 1990 shows that the term "post-conflict reconstruction" either did not appear or was used ad hoc to refer to activities during specific periods such as the post-colonial, post-World War II and post-communism eras.[4]

Thereafter, it took more than a decade to institutionalize both post-conflict reconstruction and peacebuilding in practice as well as in theory. A turning point came when the United Nations Peacebuilding Commission was created with resolution 60/180 and resolution 1645 (2005) of Dec. 20, 2005. The Commission was explicitly charged, among other things, with "advising on and proposing integrated strategies for post-conflict peacebuilding and recovery." The creation of the Commission reflected a commitment by the international community to undertake sustained engagement in countries emerging from conflict.

In 2005, the UN Peacebuilding Commission was established

On Oct. 11, 2006, the United Nations also launched the Peacebuilding Fund, which relied on voluntary contributions from Member States to finance the Peacebuilding Commission. With the creation of both the Commission and the Fund, post-conflict reconstruction became firmly linked with peacebuilding, while at the same time, questions began to arise about the nature and scope of the peacebuilding process.

---

[4] The first initiative in carving out post-conflict reconstruction as a niche of its own came in July 1992, when the Secretary-General at the time, Boutros Boutros-Ghali, presented his "Agenda for Peace" to the Security Council. He said, "The Council has specifically requested that I consider: preventive diplomacy, peacemaking and peace-keeping—to which I have added a closely related concept, post-conflict peace-building" (United Nations 1992).

"Post-conflict reconstruction" continues to lack a precise definition due to the complexity of post-conflict situations

It is commonly assumed that the post-conflict period starts after a peace agreement has been signed

Yet, signing a peace agreement does not necessarily qualify a country as "post-conflict" as conflict often continues

The United Nations was not alone in recognizing that post-conflict situations present special challenges and require special remedies. In 1997, the World Bank issued its *Framework for World Bank Involvement in Post-Conflict Reconstruction*, and to implement the framework, it established the Post-Conflict Fund in the newly created Conflict Prevention and Reconstruction Unit. Another fund targeting fragile and conflict-affected countries, called the Low-Income Countries under Stress Trust Fund, was also set up in the same unit in 2004.

Meanwhile, in 1995, the International Monetary Fund, which is mostly geared towards crisis lending and short-term stabilization of economic imbalances, introduced a new financing instrument for post-conflict countries, focusing on technical assistance to help its members with institution-building. The Organisation for Economic Co-operation and Development (OECD) likewise took up post-conflict peacebuilding within a larger policy framework linking conflict and development. It created the OECD Development Assistance Committee (DAC). In 1997 it then established a task force to coordinate individual donor innovations and a collective response. A Conflict Prevention and Post-Conflict Reconstruction Network of 30 units was set up in tandem to apply the DAC guidelines, which started an era of convergence between conflict prevention and peacebuilding.

Despite taking up post-conflict reconstruction as a distinctive activity, no international organization provided a precise definition of the term. The World Bank chose to associate "post-conflict" mostly with "transitional" countries undergoing their first elections after a violent conflict. Consequently, the Bank's post-conflict assistance programs consisted mainly of developing the economic infrastructure and supporting lending for social services with a view towards future investments (Flores and Nooruddin 2007). The United Nations equated post-conflict situations simply with the aftermath of war, without specifying exactly when that was. One rule of thumb, however, was that while conflict cases were associated with humanitarian relief, peacemaking and peacekeeping activities by the United Nations, post-conflict activities almost unequivocally involved peacebuilding, understood as the "full range of non-military commitments undertaken to assist countries to achieve self-sustaining peace and socio-economic development" (Tschirgi 2004, p. 2).

Clearly, therefore, "post-conflict" did not lend itself to easy definitions. One problem was defining "conflict"—determining if violent

Table I.2 **Post-conflict reconstruction from a process-oriented perspective**

Peace milestones	Possible indicators of progress
Cessation of hostilities and violence	– Reduction in the number of conflict fatalities – Reduction in the number of violent attacks – Time passed since major fighting stopped
Single political/ peace agreements	– Signing of and adherence to cease fire agreements – Signing and implementation of a comprehensive political agreement, which addresses the causes of the conflict – Endorsement of peace/political agreement by all major factions and parties to the conflict
Demobilisation, disarmament and reintegration	– No. of weapons handed in – No./proportion of combatants released from active duty and returned to barracks – No. of military barracks closed – Successfulness of reinsertion programs for ex-combatants – Reduction in total number of active soldiers/combatants – Spending cuts on military procurements
Refugee repatriation	– No./proportion of displaced persons and refugees that have returned home voluntarily – No. of displaced persons and refugees still living involuntarily in refugees centres within conflict country or abroad
Establishing a functioning state	– The extent to which impunity and lawlessness have been reduced – The extent to which the rule of law is introduced and maintained – The extent to which corruption has been reduced – Tax revenue as a proportion of GDP
Achieving reconciliation and social integration	– Number of violent incidents between groups – Perceptions of "others" (via surveys) – Extent of trust (via surveys)
Economic recovery	Economic growth recovery Increased revenue mobilization Restoring of economic infrastructure Increased foreign direct investment

Source: Brown, Langer and Stewart (2008), table 1.

conflict can be equated with war, and if so, what type and extent of war. The second problem was delineating when a conflict starts and ends. Countless documents on conflict cases talked about pre-conflict, conflict and post-conflict phases without defining those periods or even identifying them consistently.

Post-conflict reconstruction is defined in terms of milestones and progress indicators

Table I.2 outlines the process of post-conflict reconstruction in terms of milestones and progress indicators. This approach defines "post-conflict reconstruction" indirectly by focusing on the main activities undertaken in the process.

The prevailing view among conflict epxerts is that the post-conflict period starts after a peace agreement has been signed. Yet there is also awareness that signing a peace agreement does not necessarily qualify a country as post-conflict, because conflict often continues irregardless, albeit in a disguised form.

Experience shows that post-conflict countries are almost always plagued by population displacements, damaged infrastructure, reduced productive capacity, devastated government revenue base, seriously weakened human and social capital, and greatly reduced security (World Bank 2005). The main activities in the early post-conflict phase often consist of (i) demobilization and reintegration of ex-combatants, (ii) reintegration of displaced populations, and (iii) demining as a prerequisite for the normalization of civilian life and the start of development activities. Later phases of post-conflict reconstruction include institution- and capacity-building activities, including the engendering, maintenance and strengthening of the rule of law, effective governance, social policymaking and economic development.

The first phase of post-conflict reconstruction coincides with the early phase of peacebuilding

The first phase of post-conflict reconstruction coincides with the early phase of peacebuilding, originally defined as "non-military or civilian dimension of efforts to support *countries emerging from conflict*." Since its conception in the 1990s, peacebuilding has gradually become a catchall concept encompassing preventive diplomacy, preventive development, conflict prevention, conflict resolution and post-conflict reconstruction. In fact, the 2000 "Report of the Panel on United Nations Peace Operations," also known as the Brahimi Report, acknowledged the growing interlinkages between conflict and peace and adopted a longer-term view of peacebuilding, as epitomized in its doctrinal shift away from international civilian policing to rule-of-law teams. However, the emphasis in this report, as in other United Nations documents since 2000, is on the need to take a more in-depth view of peacebuilding that focuses on the structural causes of conflict.

Like the Brahimi Report, a 2004 report by the Secretary-General's High-level Panel on Threats, Challenges and Change (United Nations 2004a) put special emphasis on policies for preventing conflict, underlining that development is a condition for security and peace rather than a mere consequence. The 2004 report, however, went a step further to enumerate and discuss the emerging threats to peace and security, which include poverty; infectious disease and environmental degradation; nuclear, radiological, chemical and biological weapons;

terrorism; and transnational organized crime. To counter these threats, the report discussed deploying military capacities as a means of peace-keeping and peace enforcement.

The report suggested that peacebuilding, by contrast, involves rebuilding shattered societies. "Successful peacebuilding," it said, "requires the deployment of peacekeepers with the right mandates and sufficient capacity to deter would-be spoilers; funds for demobilization and disarmament, built into peacekeeping budgets; ... rehabilitation and reintegration of combatants, as well as other early reconstruction tasks; and a focus on building State institutions and capacity, especially in the rule of law" (United Nations 2004b, p. 5). Thus the report focused on the activities and objectives of peacebuilding undertaken under the banner of post-conflict reconstruction, which it associated mainly with the dominance of non-military efforts:

- re-establishing the conditions for self-sustaining human development with or without the help of peacekeeping forces,
- managing the major risk factors of conflict relapse, including unemployment, poverty, socioeconomic gaps and political imbalances in the institutional structures, and
- undertaking a long-term perspective on building the institutions of State and society.

The United Nations Development Programme, in a recent publication titled *Post-Conflict Economic Recovery*, characterizes post-conflict countries according to their progress along a range of "peacebuilding milestones". The report states:

> *A post-conflict country should be seen as lying somewhere along a continuum on each of these milestones, recognizing that it could sometimes move backwards. As long as a country does not slip back on too many of these milestones at once, it can reasonably be expected to continue towards recovery. The following are the most important peacebuilding milestones:*
> - Ceasing hostilities and violence;
> - Signing of peace agreements;
> - Demobilization, disarmament and reintegration;
> - Return of refugees and internally displaced persons (IDPs);
> - Establishing the foundations for a functioning State;
> - Initiating reconciliation and societal integration; and
> - Commencing economic recovery. (UNDP 2008, p. xviii)

A post-conflict country should be seen as lying somewhere along a continuum of peacebuilding milestones, recognizing that it could sometimes move backwards

Table I.3 **Post-conflict activity by the United Nations: Key concepts**

Peacemaking	Peacemaking is "action to bring hostile parties to agreement, essentially through such peaceful means as those foreseen in Chapter VI of the Charter of the United Nations; Pacific Settlement of Disputes" (United Nations 1992). In this sense, peacemaking is a diplomatic effort to promote the forging of a settlement between disputing parties.
Peacekeeping	The term "peacekeeping" is not found in the United Nations Charter and defies simple definition. "Peacekeeping" refers to a United Nations presence in the field (normally involving civilian and military personnel) that, with the consent of the conflicting parties, implements or monitors arrangements relating to the control of conflicts and their resolution, or ensures the safe delivery of humanitarian relief. Peacekeeping can be divided into three broad categories: (i) assistance in maintenance of cease-fires, (ii) implementation of comprehensive settlements, and (iii) protection of humanitarian operations. As the United Nations Peacekeeping website explains, "today's peacekeepers undertake a wide variety of complex tasks, from helping to build sustainable institutions of governance, to human rights monitoring, to security sector reform, to the disarmament, demobilization and reintegration of former combatants" (see: *www.un.org/Depts/dpko/dpko*).
Peacebuilding	Peacebuilding is associated with the transition from the end of a conflict to the attainment of lasting peace and sustainable development. The term "peacebuilding" came into widespread use after 1992 following the former United Nations Secretary General's Agenda for Peace (United Nations, 1992). According to the Secretary-General's High-level Panel on Threats, Challenges and Change, peacebuilding involves "deployment of peacekeepers with the right mandates and sufficient capacity to deter would-be spoilers; enough funds for demobilization and disarmament, built into peacekeeping budgets; … rehabilitation and reintegration of combatants, as well as other early reconstruction tasks; and a focus on building State institutions and capacity, especially in the rule of law" (United Nations 2004b, p. 5). And in a press release issued July 23, 2009, Secretary-General Ban Ki-moon said, "Building peace is about much more than ending war. It is about putting in place the institutions and trust that will carry people forward into a peaceful future".
Post-conflict reconstruction	Post-conflict reconstruction, which overlaps conceptually with post-conflict peacebuilding, involves the reconstruction of the core functions of the State and the delivery of basic public goods that support economic growth and human development.

While post-conflict peacebuilding might overlap with peacekeeping activities, there is no doubt that it extends to the processes of building and strengthening State institutions

While post-conflict peacebuilding might overlap with peacekeeping activities, there is no doubt that it extends to the processes of building and strengthening State institutions. Post-conflict peacebuilding, in other words, does not end with the establishment of nascent government structures, including the immediate transition of authority to the new government; its "nuts and bolts" start there.

Table I.3 provides details about how the United Nations defines "peacemaking", "peacekeeping", "peacebuilding" and "post-conflict reconstruction". To sum up, however, post-conflict reconstruction (i) is part of the progression from peacekeeping to peacebuilding, (ii) can include both at times, if conflict continues even after the signing of a peace agreement, and (iii) transpires as a comprehensive, multidimensional and long-term undertaking to build institutions and promote good governance after the signing of peace agreements.

Phases of post-conflict reconstruction

It is important to underline that post-conflict situations are heterogeneous in nature. Depending on the past and present government institutions, structures, practices and leadership capacities, the extent and the degree of reconstruction vary greatly, as does the length of each phase of reconstruction. In cases of severe violence and destruction, policymakers face especially daunting challenges. Kauzya (2002) points out that in Rwanda, for example, after the 1994 genocide, the public administration system was completely destroyed and could not be reformed; it had to be rebuilt. Similarly, in Timor-Leste and in Kosovo, the United Nations had to intervene to re-establish public administration. In other cases, however, where relatively strong institutions existed before the outbreak of violence, reform and reconfiguration would be most appropriate.

Post-conflict reconstruction is part of the progression from peacekeeping to peacebuilding

Since countries emerging from violent conflict present unique circumstances that require different approaches for strengthening public administration, the term "post-conflict reconstruction" encompasses a range of activities. These take place in four main phases:

It can include both at times, if conflict continues even after the signing of a peace agreement

- **Emergency relief:** Meeting the population's immediate aid needs, often through massive external technical, financial, logistical and social assistance from external sources;
- **Rehabilitation:** Rehabilitating basic infrastructure, structures, facilities, equipment, logistics and basic human capacities;
- **Reform and modernization of the State:** Redesigning institutions, systems, structures, human capacities, etc., to improve effectiveness and efficiency and to control costs; and
- **Reconfiguration of the role of the State:** Redesigning public administration to include the governed (civil society, private sector) at all levels (Kauzya, 2002).

These phases are not always sequential; they generally overlap because the process of rebuilding public administration is multidirectional. In other words, it is probably not possible to complete emergency relief before starting rehabilitation, just as it is not possible to complete rehabilitation before starting reform. Even the process of reconfiguring the public administration system to make it more inclusive, responsive and accountable to the community cannot wait until the reform phase is complete. Nonetheless, the phases need to be conceptualized as distinct because some aspects should not be mixed.

Post-conflict reconstruction is a comprehensive, multidimensional and long-term undertaking to build institutions and promote good governance after the signing of peace agreements

Emergency relief and rehabilitation of infrastructure, facilities, and capacities are the first phases of post-conflict reconstruction

- **Emergency relief.** In the immediate aftermath of conflict, the stakeholders are not yet organized in a stable way, emotionally or materially, to effectively participate in the rethinking and re-design of the public administration. At this stage, the public administration itself is almost non-existent, the private sector is often destroyed and civil society is in disarray. Tensions that may have triggered the conflict in the first place and/or arisen as a result are too high to permit rational debate on reconfiguring public administration. Metaphorically, this is a stage when fires must be put out and anyone with a bucket of water is welcomed. In other words, the focus is on providing food, shelter, medical care, financial assistance, etc.

Emergency relief ensures the survival of a country and its people

- **Rehabilitation.** This phase in most cases involves repairing buildings and other facilities and putting structures and systems back in place to permit orderly administration and decision-making. It also includes reassembling human resources and training them to staff the rehabilitated structures and systems. The rehabilitation stage should prepare the country to participate in a deep and engaged debate on the future of the country's public administration. The problem with this phase is that in most cases there is a lack of long-range planning. Authorities are preoccupied with putting back structures that may, in just a few years, have to be dismantled as reform and reconfiguration take place. In most cases, successful rehabilitation will end with adequate administrative institutions such as functioning legislatures, ministries, and judicial systems. However, most of these institutions and structures will be inefficient because of inadequate human capacities and systems. Also the linkages among them will be weak if there was little collaboration during the rehabilitation process. Sometimes individual donors or development partners support the rehabilitation of individual institutions. Where these have not collaborated, it is possible to have two institutions in the same country following contradictory systems.

- **Reform and modernization of the State.** The reform phase involves the rethinking of systems, procedures, organizational structures, human capacities, information management, methodologies and institutional linkages as they relate to the entire development process. In other words, reform "is a process of re-adjustment of State institutions and public management to the need for greater cost-effectiveness, quality, simplicity and transparency" (Alberti 2005, p. 10). The biggest preoccupation during reform is efficiency. In most cases, reforms have come as packages conceived of elsewhere and branded "best practices". Rarely have reforms been home-grown in response to local needs. Consequently, reform efforts are often ill-suited to the situation at hand. For example, some efforts focus on downsizing the public service even when the country has too few personnel already. There have also been cases of countries being hurried to privatize enterprises before the social ownership of such enterprises has been sorted out.

- **Reconfiguration of the role of the State.** This phase involves intensive self-examination and strategic planning for the country. It is the phase that often lasts longest, depending on the readiness of the country's leadership and people to engage in participatory rethinking and re-engineering of the country's governance and public administration. This phase will resolve issues such as participatory governance, private-sector development, the extent of civil society's involvement as a strong partner in governance, and the extent of partnerships among government, the private sector and civil society at all levels (community, local, national, regional and international). During reconfiguration, a country reaffirms that participatory governance is a shared responsibility, and engages with global actors and the forces of globalization in the country's development. It also acts assertively to anchor governance and public administration to its own needs and circumstances.

Modernization of the State and reconfiguration of the state's role are the next steps in the reconstruction process

The four phases of post-conflict reconstruction can be summarized as follows: emergency relief ensures the survival of a country and its people, rehabilitation restores some form of administration, reform strives to make public administration efficient, and reconfiguration of the role of the State installs governance. Each phase of post-conflict reconstruction thus has a particular focus: emergency relief is about short-term recovery, rehabilitation centers on creating a framework for public administration, reform emphasizes public management, and reconfiguration centers on good governance.

It is worth reiterating that each country's experience with these phases strongly depends on its specific circumstances—the nature of the conflict it has undergone, the extent to which public administration has been affected and the level of commitment by local forces to putting the country back on the road to development. ◆

3. Goals of public adminison reconstruction after conflict

Post-conflict reconstruction goals include ensuring peace and security, fostering social reconciliation and cohesion, and promoting socio-economic development

Generally speaking, there are three major goals for national reconstruction in post-conflict situations: (i) ensuring peace and security; (ii) fostering social reconciliation and cohesion and respect for human rights; and (iii) promoting socio-economic development. These coincide with the three pillars of the United Nations' work—peace and security issues, human rights protection, and development efforts. Development is not possible "without peace and security, but successful development also contributes to peace and security by reducing some of the tensions that give rise to conflict. Although there are two way interactions between peace and development, resolving conflict and avoiding violence within a society are necessary preconditions for development" (United Nations 2007c, p. 14). Likewise if governments do not guarantee the respect of universal human rights, tensions among different interest groups, including majority and minority groups, are more likely to escalate into violence and threaten peace and security, thus endangering development as well.

We should not forget that the overriding purpose for developing democratic governments is to enable them to support peace and security, social harmony and development. Achieving these goals requires appropriate leadership capacities, governance mechanisms and public administration institutions and processes. The State's fundamental functions include guaranteeing personal security and property, providing for the common defence, ensuring law and order, protecting and maintaining human rights and freedoms, promoting the general welfare, creating an enabling environment for economic development, and promoting social justice. Without security ensured by the State, there is no order; without justice administered by appropriate courts, there is no certainty of law and security; without basic health services and sanitation delivered by the public sector, there is suffering and limited life expectancy; without an enabling environment for economic development, there is no future and no peace.

Therefore, providing effective services to the population is the most critical challenge in post-conflict situations. The State's ability to provide essential public services, especially security and justice, can advance the peacebuilding process and prevent relapses into violence. As a recent United Nations report notes, "people will most likely trust government when public servants effectively deliver the desired services in a timely manner, behave transparently with accountability and integrity, act in an ethical manner, are responsive to the needs of the people, and can be identified with the people they serve. Above all, in a post-conflict and crisis situation the public service must be seen to be fundamentally and positively different from the previous government in all its respects" (United Nations 2007a).

Ensuring peace and security

There is a growing awareness among United Nations Member States that for peace to be sustainable, it has to rest on a sovereign State's capacity to resolve conflicts by means other than war (Schnabel and Ehrhart 2005). In post-conflict societies, the remnants of wartime military and security apparatuses pose great risks to internal security: inflated armies with little or no civilian control; irregular and paramilitary forces; an overabundance of arms and ammunition in private and government hands; weak internal security forces; and a lack of trust in the government's control over police and military forces (Schnabel and Ehrhart 2006). Therefore, public administration institutions must be designed or redesigned so that security institutions include an effective and accountable police body. In addition, the military must be depoliticized and unified, and civilian combatants must be disarmed and demobilized.

Fostering social reconciliation

To recover from violent conflict, States must promote psychological healing and social reconciliation. As Karbo and Mutisi (2008, p. 2) note, "those who have experienced the horrors of violent conflict are often scarred emotionally and left traumatized ... Healing at the psychological level allows for the rebuilding and mending of broken relationships, which is necessary for the human society to remain intact. Scholars and practitioners contend that psychosocial healing is an effective way to reconstruct and rebuild society with an improved quality of life".

To achieve social reconciliation, States must ensure respect for human rights, particularly minority rights; promote redistributive policies and social justice; include diversity management in public administration; and establish truth commissions (with the caveat that peace and security come before justice, and temporal distance is needed to

States must promote psychological healing and social reconciliation through respect for human rights, particularly minority rights; redistributive policies and social justice

close open wounds). Governments need to provide and ensure access to essential services—including security, justice, health, education, sanitation and basic infrastructure—to all groups in society. At the same time, the State also needs to provide an enabling framework for economic development. There is little chance that disarming and de-mobilizing armed militia will be long-lasting unless ex-combatants can make a living and access resources without using force.

Strengthening civil society institutions and making sure that societal groups take part in decisions that affect their lives are critical elements for ensuring peace agreements' sustainability. Citizen engagement in policy-making allows diverse values and interests to be brought forward.[5] How-ever, a strong and vocal civil society is not enough for successful recon-struction and peacebuilding. Another necessary component is effective use of information and communication technologies and knowledge management. A recent United Nations publication puts it this way:

> *Access to reliable and objective information is a vital element of democratic process and settings. Countries' experience shows that the manipulation of information can be a trigger of rising misunderstanding and tensions that can lead to devastating con-flicts. Therefore, the promotion of exchange and dissemination of information is an important element of re-construction efforts. It is therefore in the interest of governments to set up mechanisms allowing them to manage information and knowledge assets. (United Nations 2007b, p. 19).*

Promoting socio-economic development

Only by shifting the energies and focus of the population from conflict to development can a country avoid relapsing into violence

As stated earlier in this chapter, development is a necessary condition for peace and security. In post-conflict situations, it is only by shifting the energies and focus of the population from conflict to development that a country can avoid relapsing into violence.

Douglas North, a winner of the Nobel Prize in economics in 1993, has concluded that economic growth is related not only to technological or demographic factors, but also—and more impor-tantly—to institutional factors. To foster socio-economic develop-ment in countries emerging from violent conflict, one key challenge is macroeconomic reconstruction and stabilization. Regulating owner-ship in a post-conflict society and combating and constraining the so-called "war economies" and parallel economies are fundamental pri-

---

[5] See also United Nations (2007a).

orities. In the immediate period after the end of violence, it is crucial to create jobs through public works programmes and to stimulate micro and small enterprises. Threatened livelihoods can easily lead to a new outbreak of conflicts. Reintegrating ex-combatants, refugees and internally displaced people into the economy can further strain the finances of fragile post-conflict States already suffering from sharply reduced revenues. Declining confidence in the domestic currency leads to brain drain and dwindling capital, and thus to a spiral of continued economic failures.

It is crucial to create jobs through public works programmes and to stimulate micro and small enterprises, and to re-integrate ex-combatants into the economy

To encourage the development of market mechanisms that can efficiently and effectively allocate scarce economic resources, new macroeconomic policies and institutions are needed, along with capacity-building for people working in these areas. International organizations should encourage governments to establish sustainable partnerships with the private sector (public-private partnerships) and to foster private sector development.

In addition to macroeconomic stabilization, other factors are important for socio-economic development. These include reconstructing economic institutions, including property rights; dismantling the economy of violence (through security sector reforms and provision of economic opportunities for ex-combatants); and promoting social justice through distributive policies. ◆

Countries in post conflict situations must rebuild trust and legitimacy in government institutions

4. Challenges in reconstructing public administration after conflict

After violent conflict, countries face a number of unique challenges in rebuilding their public administration systems to achieve the goals outlined above—ensuring peace and security, fostering social reconciliation, and promoting development. Among other things, countries must rebuild trust and legitimacy in government institutions, re-establish the rule of law and justice, and build a political culture that emphasizes institutionalized political competition as opposed to violent confrontation and personalized politics. Success depends largely on the effectiveness of public administration. In most cases, however, the public administration that is supposed to enact reforms

Success depends largely on the effectiveness of public administration to deliver public services

is the same one that contributed, either directly or indirectly, to the original conflict. Reconstruction, therefore, is a complex task that requires effective leadership.

The main challenges in rebuilding public administration after conflict include:

- Developing effective public sector leadership;
- Building effective public administration institutions;
- Strengthening human resources in the public sector;
- Establishing mechanisms for inclusive governance; and
- Improving the delivery of public services.

These challenges are discussed briefly below, and each is then explored in depth in a subsequent chapter. The assumption is that stronger public administration will lead to two critical outputs: better provision of public services and enhanced trust in government. Achieving these will ultimately solidify peace and level the playing field for all actors to engage in development.

Developing effective public sector leadership

It is not possible to transform public administration without transforming the beliefs, attitudes and behaviours of political leaders and civil servants so that they perform effectively within a democratic setting. Leadership with a vision of the future is fundamental in implementing institutional reforms. Competent leaders must also be able to mobilize the people around them to move reforms in the right direction and achieve shared goals.

Leadership and institutional development are symbiotic. Leaders create institutions, but they must also be willing to submit to the authority of these same institution

Leadership and institutional development are symbiotic. Leaders create institutions, but they must also be willing to submit to the authority of these same institutions. Unless leaders champion the creation and operationalization of the right institutions, no lasting peace can be guaranteed. Weak government institutions (or low levels of institutionalization) often lead to violent conflict as different factions vie for power. With capable leadership, however, conflict is channeled through the appropriate political and legal institutions.

Building effective public institutions

In post-conflict situations, comprehensive institutional development is often necessary. Political institutions, for example, might require reform—changes in the political-party system, perhaps, or constitutional reforms that guarantee rights to minorities and create checks and balances to prevent abuses of power. Similarly, market institutions—property rights, regulatory frameworks, banking systems, etc.—might need to be overhauled. Civil society institutions, too, might require attention. This report, however, focuses solely on rebuilding public administration institutions.

In post-conflict situations, creating effective public administration is not simply a matter of reconstructing institutions according to traditional models. Instead, leaders may need to remodel the old institutions or search for new forms that fit the country's unique needs, taking account of its cultural, historical and political reality.

An important challenge facing government leaders and development partners alike is how to restructure the public service in an inclusive, transparent and comprehensive way so that it incorporates and reinvigorates desirable traditional public service values, such as impartiality, integrity, and dedication. It is only through a public service based upon such values that citizens can be served while management innovations and efficiency improvements can be promoted to encourage more open and responsive forms of administration. This virtuous cycle of effective service delivery and open administration can then act as a vigorous counterforce against any backsliding to conflict or violence.

An additional challenge is making sure that the public servants themselves are invested in the change process so that they can become the most effective contributors to and champions of their country's recovery. The composition and functioning of the public service represents a microcosm of the society and mirrors the larger governance environment.

Creating effective public administration is not simply a matter of reconstructing "old" institutions

Instead, leaders may need to remodel the old institutions or search for new forms that fit the country's unique needs taking account of its cultural, historical and political reality

Strengthening human resources in the public sector

Another critical challenge is how the capacities, beliefs, attitudes and behaviors of civil servants can be transformed so that they can operate effectively within a democratic institutional setting where conflict is channeled through appropriate political and legal institutions. It is not possible to transform public administration without a transformation of the beliefs, attitudes and behaviors of people and how they relate to each other and their capacities for positive engagement.

Establishing mechanisms for inclusive governance

Another important element in ensuring that countries emerging from conflict do not relapse into violence is to ensure that all social groups are part of the country's transformation process. The greatest challenges in building participatory governance are developing appropriate mechanisms for the articulation of citizens' interests and developing a culture of pluralism. If institutions are created without any mechanisms for expressing citizens' concerns and mobilizing grassroots participation, then the institutions remain empty shells.

Decentralization can help people become engaged in managing public affairs and committed to peaceful progress

Decentralization can help people become engaged in managing public affairs and committed to peaceful progress. Under other circumstances, decentralization can exacerbate local conflicts and undermine sustainable peace. Once again, the challenge for countries in post-conflict situations is to figure out which mechanisms best suit their own situation based on their past, present and future capacities and expectations.

Providing citizen-centric public service delivery

Transforming the beliefs, attitudes, and behaviours of civil servants is of paramount importance to post-conflict reconstruction

Running a government is largely about ensuring that basic services, such as security, sanitation, health care, education and justice, get to those who need them. To accomplish this, healthy democracies require fair and efficient public administration—nationally and locally—with a solid civil service and equitable social policies (UNDP 2008).

In post-conflict situations, the provision of efficient and affordable public services for all, including vulnerable groups and minorities, remains a core function of the State, but in the wake of severely diminished human, financial and material resources, it becomes harder than ever. At the same time, it becomes more important than ever, not only for sustaining the population, but also for restoring public trust in government and keeping the peace. ▪

Chapter II

Developing Effective Public Sector Leadership

One of the most critical elements for the success of post-conflict reconstruction is the presence of capable leaders, at all levels of government, who are committed to transforming conflict into peaceful coexistence and collaboration. Yet as energy is exerted on peace negotiations, peacekeeping operations and basic humanitarian assistance, too little attention is paid to cultivating effective leaders and promoting respect for institutions. Instead, the conversation is dominated by discussion about how parties to the conflict should share power and wealth. This approach often reignites conflict, demonstrating the need to focus more sharply on leadership transformation and capacity-building.

This chapter looks at the challenges in building effective leadership, the capacities needed by post-conflict leaders and strategies for developing those capacities. The chapter also analyzes the role of international and regional donors in promoting leadership capacity development.

1. Challenges in reconstructing public sector leadership

Every country strives for high-quality leadership in public administration. For post-conflict countries, however, special challenges may arise because of weak governance institutions, the difficulty of institutionalizing new leadership models, and discrepancies between formal rules and actual behaviours.

Overcoming weak governance structures and unpredictable systems

The root causes of intrastate conflict are usually assumed to be poverty and economic inequality or clashes among different ethnic or religious groups. However, the central cause of violent conflict is weak governance institutions characterized by low levels of institutionalization and the personalization of politics. This is also one reason for relapses into conflict after peace agreements have been signed and governance and public administration institutions redesigned. In other words, divisive politics based on the monopolization of power and the exclusion of major social and political groups in the pre-conflict stage is often responsible for armed rebellion and civil wars.

As an example, consider Uganda. Rebel groups there took up arms in response to a succession of dictatorial regimes whose leaders repressed the opposition and were accused of rigging the 1980 general elections (Langseth and Mugaja, 1996). In Rwanda, a succession of Hutu-dominated governments that expelled and excluded Tutsis triggered a Tutsi-led armed rebellion and the Hutus' subsequent efforts to exterminate the Tutsi in the 1994 genocide. In Somalia, Siad Barre monopolized power from 1969 until 1991 by favoring his own clan and imprisoning and killing opponents. Therefore, a major priority of post-conflict governance is to transform previous patterns of divisive oppositional politics.

While many conflict-affected countries have elaborate constitutions, charters, criminal and civil codes and justice systems, their institutions, including the rule of law, are nevertheless often undermined by a culture of personalized politics, corruption and impunity for the powerful. Recent scholarship indicates that communal divisions within the State are often actively crafted by political elites, community leaders or

The root causes of intrastate conflict are usually assumed to be poverty and economic inequality or ethic/religious clashes, however, the central cause of violent conflict is weak governance institutions

Institutions are often undermined by a culture of personalized politics, corruption and impunity for the powerful

In some conflict-prone countries, the personalization of power and the neo-patrimonial nature of the State have led to institutional decay rather than development

ethnic activists who seek to band a community together to compete for scarce resources, access to State power or other instrumental gains (Horowitz 2000; Brass 1991; Connor 1994; Kaufman 2001; Lake and Rothchild 1996; Fearon and Laitin 2004). In some conflict-prone countries, the personalization of power and the neo-patrimonial nature of the State have led to institutional decay rather than development. By definition, a neo-patrimonial system develops when political actors do not recognize the State as an institution and when the power to rule resides in a person rather than an office. There is no division between public and private spheres, as these two coincide in one person (the dictator) or in a specific group of people. Thus there are no formal mechanisms for political competition or political participation. Instead, politics is practised as a zero-sum game, in which the gains of one group translate to losses for other groups. The State's inability to function effectively, let alone achieve economic and social progress, breeds conflict and violence as competing factions vie for power and control of resources.

In post-conflict situations, a committed leadership needs to be in place to champion institutional development

In many countries that have experienced violent conflict, institutional decay can be attributed to leaders who thrived on promoting a personality cult, clientelism, nepotism and repression of dissent. How then can leaders be part of the solution to the challenge of rebuilding an effective and equitable public administration? How can the gap between government institutional prescriptions and actual leaders' behaviour be bridged? In order to tackle these questions, we examine more carefully the challenges of institutionalization, the capacities that have proven most effective for leaders in post-conflict situations and the strategies and tools available to build them.

Obstacles to institutionalizing new models of leadership

There has been a longheld assumption that designing the right institutions is all that counts, but for institutions to matter, their underlying rules and values must be respected by leaders and all other constituents

In post-conflict situations, a committed leadership needs to be in place to champion institutional development. As already mentioned, designing appropriate institutions is a complex and challenging task but an essential ingredient for recovery. However, it is only the first step in the quest for sustainable peace and development. There has been a long-held assumption that designing the right institutions is all that counts, and that new rules, processes and technologies automatically replace the old order. Yet the new message of reform is unlikely to sink in or make much difference if it does not fully reckon with old mindsets and traditional practices. For institutions to matter, their underlying rules and values must be respected by leaders and all other constituents.

Formal rules are easily changed by writing new rules, but beliefs, informal codes of conduct, ingrained behaviours and informal constraints are much more difficult to change. Because reformers, including the donor community, sometimes have only a partial understanding of local institutions, their efforts at reform do not always bring about the desired results. Modifying only the visible structure of institutional systems cannot by itself change how actors behave. New rules that are simply grafted onto old superstructures or insensitively imposed from outside are doomed to fail (Alberti and Balogun, 2005). This does not imply that the past dictates the future and that no changes are possible. What it means instead is that past behaviours and beliefs should always be taken into consideration when embarking on institutional reforms.

Formal rules are easily changed by writing new rules, but beliefs, informal codes of conduct, ingrained behaviours and informal constraints are much more difficult to change

The same may be said when transferring institutional models from one country to another. In many instances, this has been done without consideration for pre-existing institutions and the local political culture. This was the case in a number of African countries that imported democratic institutions from the West between the late 1940s and the 1960s. As Balogun (2002) has noted, these attempts at institutional grafting ended much the same way that the earliest medical heart-transplant operations did—with the recipient's body rejecting the externally donated organs. According to Adamolekun (2005, p. 2), "the emergence of one-party and military governments in place of democratic systems ... led many observers to conclude that the transfer efforts failed".

Divergence between rules and behaviours

One of the major problems in many post-conflict situations (especially in Africa and Latin America) is the discrepancy between the formal rules for governing and the actual behaviour of leaders and civil servants. While many countries have comprehensive, well-written constitutions, government officials often fail to follow the rules therein. We do not have to look far for explanations; the problem lies in human nature. If human beings were merely passive agents, the law would suffice to keep them within institutional bounds. However, because humans exercise independent thought and judgment, they are capable of acting for private ends and taking institutions in directions that were not originally intended.

One of the major problems in many post-conflict situations is the discrepancy between the formal rules for governing and the actual behaviour of leaders and civil servants

The challenge is ensuring that governance and public administration institutions do not become total captives of dysfunctional behaviour, and certainly not captives of personalities. A constitution that

Building a viable public administration requires institutionalization of appropriate behaviour for civil servants

The more institutionalized the civil service is, the less vulnerable it is to external influences and the more integrity its members demonstrate

can be easily amended to benefit those in power is no defensible constitution, much less an institution. An institution is viable only when it retains its substance and character over time, even when personalities and circumstances change.

Building a viable public administration requires institutionalization of appropriate behaviour for civil servants. What is meant here by "institutionalization" is the process by which roles and values become internalized. This occurs when members of the institution have high levels of professionalism and identify with institutional goals. The more institutionalized the civil service is, the less vulnerable it is to external influences and the more integrity its members demonstrate. They feel empowered to act independently of other political forces while carrying out their statutory functions. The police constable apprehends offenders without waiting to be so instructed by his or her superiors. The police commissioner will not declare an assembly to be unlawful on the say-so of a high-ranking political functionary, but only in accordance with the law. An anti-corruption agency will resist the temptation to be used as a weapon to settle political scores or to harass and intimidate law-abiding citizens (Alberti and Balogun, 2005).

The problem in many post-conflict countries lies in the low level of institutionalization of governance institutions. Only when members of an organization have respect for the institutions' values and objectives will their behaviour conform to formal rules. ◆

2. Capacities needed for post-conflict leadership

Leaders in post-conflict situations need to be as able and agile as leaders of countries enjoying relative peace, but they have the added challenges of managing conflict in divided societies and overcoming the devastating effects of war and destruction. Table II.1 shows how leadership capacity development differs in the two environments. Dr. Toga McIntosh, who was appointed Minister of Planning and Economic Affairs in Liberia in February 2006, aptly described the challenges facing his country's leaders:

In a country that had normal governance processes before the conflict, the task of capacity building is easier. But our country suffered decades of bad governance resulting in collapse and civil conflict. In all

Table II.1 **Comparison of the context for capacity-development efforts in post-conflict and non-fragile States**

Similarities	Differences
− Need to consider sustainability and reinforcement of endogenous capacity	− Pressure to restore services and security quickly
− Long timeframe	− Short timeframe
− Change agents and champions, political will and ownership	− Limited formal capacity to build on, but great informal capacity to tap into
− Importance of adapting intervention templates	− Often not simply rebuilding, but creating new capacities and balancing history with needed capacities
− Systems perspective to capture complexity and interconnections	− Little trust and social capital, institutional resilience
	− Hyper-politicized environment

Source: Adapted from Brinkerhoff (2007)

areas of government we have to start from scratch. For instance, we need to put in place a justice system and develop respect for the rule of law. Furthermore, as we advance in our reform process, we must enter into continuous dialogue with all of our country's stakeholders. This means that we have to spend a lot of time and energy in seminars or in doing paper work. The problem is that people cannot eat that. We must deliver something tangible to the people quickly. That is complicated by the fact that we do not have the public sector capacities required to plan, manage and deliver services. It means that we have to proceed simultaneously with a three-pronged approach. Firstly, we need to demobilize the combatants. Secondly, we have to put in place laws and a justice system that works. Thirdly, we must focus on delivering some limited but effective basic services. These things we must accomplish within the first three years". (Greijn 2007)

In addition to producing tangible benefits, leaders in post-conflict situations must grapple with psycho-social challenges (see table II.2). This means trying "to overcome the bitterness and grievances inherent in protracted conflicts—the social distancing, mistrust, misperceptions, and mutual fears that such violence engenders among former enemies ... The goal is for former antagonists to be peacefully reintegrated into cooperative governance structures and to coexist together in a shared nation-state" (Aiken 2008, p. 4).

Understood in this way, reconciliation is a fundamentally transformative process, one that requires "changing the motivations, goals, beliefs, attitudes, and emotions of the great majority of society members regarding the conflict, the nature of the relationship between the

Reconciliation is a fundamentally transformative process, one that requires changing the motivations, goals, beliefs, attitudes, and emotions of the great majority of society members regarding the conflict

Table II.2 **Psycho-social challenges to sustainable governance**

Social challenges	Psychological challenges	Structural challenges
– Breakdown of social cohesion	– Negative stereotypes	– Severe disparities in:
– Decline of social capital	– Prejudice	- Social power
– Physical and social segregation	– Victimization and grievance	- Economic power
– Lack of communication and mistrust	– Biased myths and memories	- Political power

Source: Aiken (2008)

The first major psycho-social transformation should occur within the leadership group

parties, and the parties themselves" (Bar-Tal and Bennink 2004, p. xv). The first major psycho-social transformation should occur within the leadership group. As mentioned earlier, the attitudes and behaviours of leaders are the major factor affecting the quality and survival of governance and public administration institutions and in preventing relapses into conflict. At the same time, leaders must also work for psycho-social transformation in the society at large. This involves change at three different levels, related to the past, present and future.

In terms of the past, leaders in post-conflict environments need to address the legacies of the past in order to rebuild social cohesion. In particular, they must establish mechanisms for equal protection of rights; establish truth commissions; reinforce alternative dispute mechanisms; and launch programmes to deal with violence against vulnerable groups, including women and children.

With respect to the present, leaders must focus on reversing structural inequalities through appropriate distributive policies that redress disparities in educational levels and employment opportunities; ensure equal representation of vulnerable and marginal groups in government agencies, security forces and the judiciary; promote equal access to administrative and political positions; and ensure that all groups benefit from public services, including access to housing, health and other key services.

Fostering dialogue among all antagonistic groups and promoting a collective psycho-social transformation is a key ingredient of capable leadership

With regard to the future, leaders must create social and economic opportunities for all groups in society through development. This requires fostering dialogue among all antagonistic groups and building consensus, thus promoting a collective psycho-social transformation.

Commitment to change

The success of post-conflict reconstruction depends first and foremost on the willingness of leaders to transform their mindsets and behaviour to act in the public interest (rather than for private gain) and in accordance with institutions—impersonal rules—that have been legally established and agreed upon. Fostering a political culture that values respect for institutions is of the utmost importance. The critical issue is to move from a "personalistic" type of leadership to what Weber defined as a rational-legal, or democratic, leader—that is, a leader who is subject to the rule of law.[6]

The commitment of the leadership class to the values underpinning public administration institutions cannot be emphasized enough. By "leadership class", we mean not just high-level governmental officials, but opposition-party leaders, civic leaders and other leaders of opinion. Unless they share the institutions' underlying values (say, multiparty competition, the rule of law, separation of powers, ethics and accountability, and professionalism), the chances are that the institutions will constantly swing back and forth on the integrity scale.

The commitment of the leadership class to the values underpinning public administration institutions cannot be emphasized enough

To reverse a culture of violence and restore trust among competing factions in society, leaders must be willing to empower one another (a horizontal sharing of power) and to delegate authority to their subordinates (a hierarchical process). The State should be seen not as a network of relations built around a strongman, but as a set of functions that are to be performed in a neutral and objective way. In other words, the State cannot be treated as the property of the rulers and their clan or entourage, who are entitled to reap any benefits that it might yield. Such views must give way to a new, shared trust in impartial public institutions before which all persons are equal and entitled to equal protection under the law.

Ability to unite citizens and build a positive vision for the future

Leadership with a vision for the future is fundamental in ensuring that institutional reforms are implemented. Competent leaders who are able to mobilize the people around them to move the reforms in the right direction and to achieve public shared goals are essential (Kauzya, 2009)[7].

Leadership with a vision for the future is fundamental in ensuring that institutional reforms are implemented

Building consensus on maintaining peace and developing a culture of prevention is one of the most important tasks leaders face in the aftermath of a violent conflict. A broad range of actors must be in-

---

6 A democratic rule of law ensures "political rights, civil liberties, and mechanisms of accountability which in turn affirm the equality of all citizens and constrain potential abuses of state power" (O'Donnell 2004, p. 32).
7 The following points have been adapted from Kauzya's article on "Leadership Capacity Development Perspectives in Africa" in Pagaza I and D. Argyriades (eds.), Winning the Needed Change: Saving our Planet, IIAS, 2009.

volved in elaborating and implementing practical prevention policies that address the root causes of conflict in particular situations. This calls for a new spirit of collaboration among national and international actors and involves the development of common mechanisms for addressing potential crises in a way that takes account of the perspectives of all parties to the conflict.

Even if new institutions are established, they will deadlock if their members fail to reach consensus or compromise. Thus, leadership again is crucial and needs to model the behaviour of inclusiveness

Collaborative engagement among former antagonists depends on comprehensive human rights-related education, consensus-seeking skills, and consciously inclusive policies that are formulated and implemented with the full participation of stakeholders. Even if new institutions are established, they will deadlock if their members fail to reach consensus or compromise. Thus, leadership again is crucial and needs to model the behaviour of inclusiveness. "In a highly politicized post-conflict environment where expectations of peace are very high, the perception of an inefficient or unfair system can be highly damaging. Therefore, national leaders and their international partners must be particularly careful to convey their vision to their various constituencies, demonstrate their progress, and explain positive changes to win support for the legitimacy of the emerging order. Progress is about sequencing tasks, and credibility is gained through momentum towards the goal so that the expectations of a population can be realistically managed and the trust of citizens can be gained and consolidated. Peace must be seen as an outcome of a truly inclusive process, achieved through steady progress and providing hope for more justice, more equality and increasingly better opportunities for upward social mobility" (Lakdhar 2007, p. 7).

Successful State-building often comes down to managing diversity and competition among different groups

Most fundamentally, sustained peace requires visionary leadership in a trustful, transparent and participatory partnership with civil society. Successful State-building often comes down to managing diversity and competition among different groups without resorting to violence and authoritarianism, while providing equal political and economic opportunities to all citizens, irrespective of identity. Any post-conflict leadership needs to place the larger national interest over group interests, and resolve conflicts so that there are not victors and vanquished, but only victors and partners.

In post-conflict reconstruction, leaders also need to welcome the equal contribution of women and men and vulnerable and marginalized groups. For example, the reconstruction of public administration

Figure II.1 **Conflict transformation triangle**

Types of actors	Approaches to building peace
Top Leadership – Military/ Political/ Religious Leaders with high visibility	– Focus on high-level negotiations – Emphasises cease-fire – Led by highly visible, single mediator
Middle Range Leadership – Leaders respected in sectors – Ethnic/religious leaders – Academics/intellectuals – Humanitarian leaders/NGOs	– Problem-solving workshops – Training in conflict resolution – Peace commission – Insider-partial teams
Grassroots Leadership – Local leaders – Leaders of indigenous NGOs – Community developers – Local health officials – Refugee camp leaders	– Local peace commissions – Grassroots training – Prejudice reduction – Psychological work in postwar trauma

Affected Population

Source: Derived from John Paul Lederach, Building Peace: Sustainable Reconciliation in divided Societies. (Washington D.C.: United States Institute of Peace Press, 1997, 39

structures and processes in Rwanda after 1994 would not have been possible without including a large number of women in positions of political and social power—an innovative approach that required strong political leadership.

Of course, peacebuilding cannot be accomplished by leaders alone. Indeed, the role of leaders is to facilitate the engagement of communities in reconstruction efforts. Influential leadership must come from the top, middle and grass-roots levels—an integrated approach illustrated in Lederach's now-famous "conflict transformation triangle" (see figure II.1).

Peacebuilding cannot be accomplished by leaders alone

Political, social and religious leaders all need to be strongly committed to the interests of their country in order to develop a shared national vision and manage people's expectations. Governments should explain that the vision cannot be realized immediately, but that the country is moving forward. To the extent possible, leaders should pursue redistributive policies, as failure to do so increases the risk of violent resolution of disputes. Furthermore, although national leaders are unquestionably responsible for establishing reconstruction priorities and implementing strategies, they should seek solid partnerships with international donors in order to create and solidify viable governance structures.

Ability to foster inclusiveness and manage diversity

After violent conflict, political leaders need to ensure the inclusion of all members of the population in all aspects of socio-politico-economic development

One of the causes of violent conflict in many countries is leadership that excludes certain members of the population from participating in decision making about development. Accordingly, after violent conflict, political leaders need to ensure the inclusion of all members of the population (women, youth, the disabled, all ethnic groups, political groups, religious groups, traditional and cultural leaders, etc.) in all aspects of socio-politico-economic development.

In poor countries, the public sector is often the biggest employer, and political leaders must see that public-service jobs are open to all and filled in a fair, transparent fashion. Political leaders should take a strategic stand by making it an objective to tap the full potential of all segments of the population. In addition, they must put in place a legal framework with clear policies for managing diversity in the public service. The aim should be to create equity, fairness, and predictability, instead of leaving public servants subject to the whims of political leadership. Once the legal framework is established, political leaders must then ensure adherence to it. When leaders divert from written rules and policies, everyone else tends to follow suit, once again opening the door for exclusionary practices that will stir resentment.

Willingness to nurture future leaders

Leadership is an ongoing activity

Leadership is an ongoing activity. Leaders who emerge after conflict must understand that good leadership will not start and end with them and that public administration reforms cannot be sustained without continuous, supportive, development-oriented leadership. Thus another important task for political leaders in post-conflict countries is molding the next generation of leaders. Of course, developing future leaders is part of any leader's responsibilities. However, in countries struggling to return to peace, it is especially critical to nurture motivated, responsible young leaders who are capable of helping their countries align post-conflict demands with development visions and strategies.

The first challenge concerns succession planning—preparing for others to continue managing a country's affairs once current leaders step down or can no longer serve. One leadership expert succinctly describes the importance of grooming successors: "In the leadership relay, it makes no difference how you run, if you drop the baton" (Garlow 2002, p. 175). Another says: "Achievement comes to someone when he is able to do great things for himself. Success comes when he empowers followers to do great things with him. Significance comes when he develops leaders to do great things for him. But a legacy is created only when a person puts his organization into the position to do great things without him" (Maxwell 20020, p. 104-205).

Unfortunately, political leaders who emerge after violent conflict tend to adopt the attitude of conquerors: they consider themselves invincible and imperishable. The reality is that leaders come and go. A political leader who truly wishes to leave positive prints on the history of his or her country needs to aggressively develop an inexhaustible pool of capable leaders for the country. In this way, the reconstruction agenda for public service will be assured of sustained support.

Looking closely at a number of post-conflict countries, it is clear that developing leaders for smooth succession has not been priority. It should be emphasized that leadership is not an isolated activity done by one greatly endowed person. It is an endeavor of collective community action dependent on followers who trust the leaders enough to jointly work towards mutual goals. Confusion about who will succeed the top leaders causes mistrust to cascade through all levels of government and hinders the reconstruction of public administration. In other words, in a post-conflict situation, if the political leadership is not in order, the public service cannot be in order either.

Skill in managing citizens' expectations and communicating effectively

Managing citizens' expectations after violent conflict is one of the most important tasks for the survival of any governance system. After years of suffering and destruction, much is demanded of those in power. Unfortunately, a combination of forces—huge capacity shortcomings in the public service, a prevailing culture of corruption and the after-effects of economic disruption—usually make it impossible to meet people's expectations. Post-conflict reconstruction tends to be slow and painful, and leaders have to help the population withstand the accompanying uncertainty and frustration. The role of political leadership here is to inspire people to be hopeful but not blindly so, and to motivate them to trust in their own capacities rather than in external or divine intervention. In order for this to happen, people must be led to realistically assess the country's situation and deploy their collective energy to meet the challenges.

Managing citizens' expectations after violent conflict is one of the most important tasks for the survival of any governance system

Box II.1 **Challenges in building leadership in Sierra Leone**

Sierra Leone is a small country in West Africa, with access to the sea and extensive unexploited mineral deposits. It is better known recently for the diamonds that fueled the war from 1991 to 2001, and for the atrocities committed by the rebels during this time. The country's human development index worsened during the war, which destroyed the social fabric and the economy. All economic activity declined significantly, and some operations, such as export of commodities, ceased completely. The destruction of physical infrastructure, displacement of people, rupture of social relations, etc., left the country as a failed state with widespread poverty. The intervention of the international community (the Economic Community of West African States, the United Nations and the United Kingdom), combined with widespread civil disobedience, led to the restoration of democratically elected government in 2002.

A brief review of how political leadership has evolved in Sierra Leone may be useful. The All People's Congress (APC) led by Siaka Stevens came to power in 1968, marking a major milestone in the political history of the country. This was the first time in Sub-Saharan Africa that an opposition political party took the reins of government through the ballot box, despite a delay due to an intervening period of military rule. The APC then proceeded to consolidate power and carefully—even legally (through a referendum)—abolished the opposition in 1977. From then on, there was increasing intolerance of dissent, and outsiders were excluded from policymaking. The ruling party's dominance meant that appointments to key positions in the administration, the judiciary, the parliament and even academia were increasingly determined by affiliation to the party. However, political affiliation was a necessary but not a sufficient condition for appointment. There was always a dominant group within the party, mainly of similar ethnic origins, that inevitably doled out appointments.

Throughout the periods of non-military rule (1957–1967, 1968–1992, and 1996–1997), leaders whose appointments were politically influenced were expected to remain loyal to the political system. The result was that the majority of the leadership consisted of those who were drawn from and protected by, the party in power. To survive in the pre-conflict era, leaders had to have the "correct" political affiliation. By the time Ahmad Tejan Kabbah's post-conflict Government assumed power in 2002, the practice of patronage had become almost a tradition. The problem was that it did not necessarily yield the best talents for technical positions, and it encouraged mismanagement, inefficiency and corruption. Many highly trained and qualified personnel left Sierra Leone to seek greener pastures elsewhere. In addition, the Government's inability to restore infrastructure—electricity, roads, telecommunications and water supply—further undermined the leadership's credibility.

Some might ask whether the 10 years of conflict, following upon many years of economic decline, destroyed political leadership in Sierra Leone. The resumption of party politics after the conflict suggests that was not the case. At worst, the leadership was in hibernation during the conflict, but it converged around the goal of ending the war and repelling the rebels. The current preparations for the elections confirm that the leadership was not destroyed by the war. The old leaders still have a strong influence in the main political parties, and the new leaders emerging have not demonstrated any significant differences from their predecessors. The major change is found in the systems that have been or are now being put in place for better governance and management. Although it is still early, there are signs that these are beginning to affect patterns of behaviour. Yet the vast majority of state-run institutions are running at a loss, not providing efficient services and continuing to be led by the same people. The much-talked-about civil service reform is not yet underway.

All of this suggests that the politicized nature of administrative leadership in Sierra Leone posed serious problems to adopting and implementating the policy reforms urgently required in a post-conflict economy. The challenge is therefore how to reinvigorate and unleash the latent capacity in the public service that may have been marginalized in the process of politicization. This may well be more a matter of political will than capacity per se. Appropriate solutions can come only from good political leadership; only the well-entrenched traditional parties have the machinery to mobilize the support necessary for reform. New third parties have not done very well in the entire history of the country. To be realistic, then, the chances for effecting change are greater if the impetus emerges from within the existing parties. The best approach is to identify change agents within the current leadership and complement them with change agents from abroad.

Source: M'cleod (2007)

In this communications age, when information can be diffused globally within seconds, it is important for political leaders to send out regular information on their activities. Delays in doing so can result in the spread of poisonous rumors and distorted or false information that discredits the government. For example, in Sierra Leone, failure to maintain a continuous, structured dialogue with the population allowed the opposition and other groups to put the worst possible spin on every issue. The political leadership was too often on the defensive because of unsubstantiated charges brought by irresponsible media and the opposition. Had Sierra Leone's political leaders given priority to a well-crafted communication and information strategy, the population would have had more appreciation of the leadership's efforts and results. For more details on the leadership challenges in Sierra Leone, see box II.1.

Balanced skills and personal qualities

An effective leader anywhere will have an appropriate mix of integrative, entrepreneurial, administrative and operative skills supported by adequate knowledge, networks, good character and appropriate values and attitudes. However, leadership in post-conflict countries cannot be based on leadership archetypes from the past or on models from other countries with other conditions. Post-conflict countries need "warriors" who have the abilities, values and virtues identified above, and who are willing to fight for peace, stability and development with passion, determination, foresight and versatility. When necessary, they will be iron-fisted and bark orders to ensure strict discipline, ethics and integrity. They will be decisive and purposeful and will take responsibility for the consequences of their orders. At the same time, they will be adaptable, collaborative and innovative. Their behaviour will be exemplary, and they will be prepared to continuously learn and unlearn to ensure that the organizations they lead are responsive to evolving needs. In this way, post-conflict leaders will engineer and sustain momentum for reconstructing public administration. ◆

3. Strategies and tools for leadership capacity-building

There has always been debate about how to effect social, political and economic development within an environment where human capacities are generally inadequate. Sometimes this debate paralyses development initiatives and perpetuates poor performance in the public service. One of the prerequisites for developing leadership capacity, then, is to put in place institutional arrangements and structures that provide opportunities for leadership training. For leaders to progressively develop their management knowledge and skills, they need practice, a supportive institutional infrastructure and a conducive governance and policy environment.

Each post-conflict country's leadership has to be open-minded and look at all potential solutions to their problems

Given the diversity of politico-administrative cultures and societal environments, each post-conflict country's leadership has to be open-minded and look at all potential solutions to their problems. For example, in post-conflict Rwanda, the new political and the administrative leaders were returning exiles with no experience in running the public service. Their long-term solution was to revamp the country's management-training institutions. But to govern initially, they sought help from former public service employees, whom they did not trust, but who could at least teach them the system. Southern Sudan, too, is approaching its needs realistically. The country is not yet in a position to set up a high-level centre for executive leadership development. The best it can do for now is to set up vocational centres to train mid- and lower-level public servants under the supervision of training centers in Uganda and Kenya. Southern Sudan may also utilize private consultancy and training institutions.

The key for any government is to develop a sense of direction for the public service

The key for any government is to develop a sense of direction for the public service that takes into account the country's history, its current circumstances, its position in the global world and a realistic development strategy. In other words, situational needs should dictate the approaches, techniques, thematic content and training methods to be used to improve leadership capacity. In all cases, however, when designing, planning, implementing, monitoring and evaluating leadership development programs—whether they are short-, medium- or long-term—organizers should adopt a participatory approach involving the beneficiaries and target groups of such programs. Each target group will require a program consistent with its needs, and those needs should be identified in consultation with group members.

Some people believe that top political leaders (ministers, parliamentarians, etc.) cannot be trained and are therefore beyond leadership-building initiatives. Accepting such opinions is defeatist. With the appropriate approaches and methodologies, current and future political leaders can certainly develop their leadership capacities. In fact, the more willing that top leaders are to undergo capacity-building activities, the more likely they are to be seen as honest and realistic about their limitations and therefore worthy of public trust.

As might be expected, capacity development for post-conflict leaders involves helping them acquire managerial skills and competencies. Even more fundamentally, however, it means transforming mindsets to help leaders embrace the rule of law and the need to act within a democratic institutional framework. A spirit of collaboration must also be cultivated to prevent conflict from recurring and to promote sustainable development. Leaders and the public at large should be educated to understand that solutions reached by compromise are more rewarding in the long run than the winner-take-all outcomes associated with violence and zero-sum games.

The first priorities in building leadership capacity in post-conflict situations should be (i) transforming the zero-sum paradigm, (ii) building trust and restoring relationships, (iii) developing a consensus on the "rules of the game" and (iv) strengthening communications capacities. A variety of tools and methodologies can be applied to these tasks. Below we discuss four that have been successfully used by different training organizations: visioning workshops and simulation activities, leadership coaching, staff exchanges and peer-to-peer learning.

Post-conflict capacity development implies transforming mindsets to help leaders embrace the rule of law and act within an institutional framework

Visioning workshops and simulation activities

Visioning workshops that have been successful in the past, such as the ones undertaken in Rwanda, were led by independent third parties who facilitated conflict analysis, problem-solving and reconciliation among parties engaged in protracted conflict. Bringing antagonistic leaders together in a common space and addressing conflict from a needs-based paradigm can promote communication and lead to collaborative solutions for the future. When visioning workshops bring together different sectors (public, private and civil society), they enhance trust in government by allowing participants to share information, take ownership of objectives and understand the obstacles the government faces in its work to develop the country.

The planning of visioning workshops is done by the ministry responsible for public service, with officials charged with human resource development and personnel administration taking the lead. The style that individuals use will be based on a combination of their beliefs, values and preferences, as well as the organizational culture and norms.

Simulation activities can also help build bridges of communication among opposing groups. In simulation games, participants role-play real-life situations in a secure environment and have an opportu-

Visioning workshops and simulation activities can help build bridges of communication among opposing groups

nity to reflect on lessons learned. Simulations can be used to create empathy among antagonists, to map out collaborative strategies for the country's future development, or to train participants in conflict management, conflict resolution and conflict transformation.[8]

Leadership coaching

Personal leadership coaching is becoming one of the most popular approaches to leadership development and organizational change in both the public and the private sector

Another strategy that can enhance top leadership capacity is coaching. Personal leadership coaching is becoming one of the most popular approaches to leadership development and organizational change in both the public and the private sector. It can build self-confidence, improve listening ability, enhance teamwork and communication skills and facilitate the learning of new techniques to manage change in difficult conditions.

High-level, busy government leaders often get caught up in the demands of managing government activity. Being involved in coaching enables such leaders to formulate plans, thoughts, and ideas in a neutral environment. It is a way to reevaluate current communication and management methods and look for new ways to approach old issues and problems. Taking part in a leadership coaching program is also a way for leaders to demonstrate dedication and humility. Coaching programs involve performance monitoring, which can include 360-degree assessments (reviews in which feedback is gathered from supervisors, peers and subordinates). In post-conflict situations, when top political leaders subject themselves to such scrutiny, they set examples that break resistance to change and learning within the public sector.

The question, however, is who will serve as coaches? Is it possible to identify a pool of qualified individuals who can be relied upon to periodically coach leaders and effectively develop their capacity? We believe this should be one of the tasks of those concerned with developing leadership capacity in post-conflict situations. Coaching requires not only superior knowledge and skills; it also requires mutual trust and an established reputation. Just as most professional soccer coaches have been very successful soccer players, the best leadership coaches will be experienced leaders with knowledge, skills and a positive reputation.

Liberia is one country that has implemented coaching. The Liberia Emergency Capacity Building programme recruits a number of top-level professionals with special skills, who are compensated to

---

[8] The term "conflict management" developed in the 1960s and 1970s to describe activities, often by a third party, to temporarily reduce tensions. "Conflict resolution", coined in the mid-1980s, refers to long-term solutions that address the root causes of conflict. "Conflict transformation" involves deep levels of change in the structural aspects of conflict; it includes a preventative element and focuses on relationship-building.

spearhead reforms. Another project, called Transfer of Knowledge through Expatriate Nationals (TOKTEN), has also been launched. Managed in collaboration with the United Nations Development Programme, TOKTEN recruits expatriate Liberians to undertake specific short-term assignments that often range from three to six months. The project provides them with a return ticket and meets their local costs. Finally, Liberia has also set up the Senior Executive Service (SES), an effort to recruit 100 very competent Liberians, in batches over a three-year period, to help bolster the public sector's capacity to deliver services (Greijn 2007).

Staff exchanges and visits

Staff exchange and visits can help leaders to develop their capacities by meeting and conferring with their professional counterparts and getting first-hand experience in different ways of doing things. This is an approach that post-conflict countries can jointly promote to share experiences and gain quick learning. It is actually now a very common practice for countries emerging from conflict to seek for effective solutions to their governance and public administration challenges and for governemnt officials to visit other countries in order to learn from their experiences.

Staff exchange and visits can help leaders to develop their capacities by meeting and conferring with their professional counterparts and getting first-hand experience in different ways of doing things

Peer-to-peer learning

While staff exchanges and visits are usually one-time events, peer-to-peer learning is an ongoing process for sustainable knowledge transfer. The United Nations is increasingly focusing on peer-to-peer (or practitioner-to-practitioner) transfers because they promote technical cooperation, help match supply a or expertise and experience, and are not just donor-to-recipient exchanges. They are characterized by the following elements:

Peer-to-peer learning is an ongoing process for sustainable knowledge transfer

- Exchange of knowledge, know-how, expertise and experience between people and organizations with similar roles and responsibilities, facing similar issues and problems; and
- Decentralized cooperation that implies a demand-driven process in which one party is willing to learn and the other party is willing to share the lessons derived from its own experience, as well as to learn from the process of adaptation. People who have taken risks and conducted successful innovations are proud of what they have achieved and are usually eager to share their knowledge.

Peer-to-peer transfers may include the following elements:

- Establishment of regional and national networks of leaders and human resources managers;
- Documentation and dissemination of effective capacity development practices;
- National and international workshops;
- Dialogue among cities and/or governments;
- Training activities;
- Study tours;
- Consultation and the exchange of technical assistance; and
- Transfer or adaptation of effective practices for leadership capacity development.

South-South information sharing and cooperation are powerful tools for fostering good governance and development

In the United Nations' experience, South-South information sharing and cooperation are powerful tools for fostering good governance and development. Accordingly, General Assembly resolution 50/225 on Public Administration and Development underlines the importance of enhancing international cooperation in public administration, including South-South and interregional cooperation. Furthermore, General Assembly resolution 57/277 of December 2002 recommends that particular attention be devoted to the exchange of experience related to public administration. In its resolution A/62/7, the General Assembly also encourages governments to strengthen national programmes devoted to the promotion and consolidation of democracy, including through increased bilateral, regional and international cooperation, taking into account innovative approaches and best practices. ◆

4. The role of external partners in building leadership capacity

Institutions imposed without local participation and support are not sustainable. Devoid of local ownership, capacity-building undertakings tend to ignore the history and value systems of the country in question—a recipe for fueling conflict rather than preventing it. Therefore, capacity development requires in-depth knowledge and understanding of specific country contexts.

The United Nations development agenda advocates national ownership of country strategies. In other words, each country must be free to determine its own development strategy. This is particularly important for the recovery of public administration and governance after a conflict. In the immediate aftermath of conflict, international actors may be needed to deliver emergency and relief aid in humanitarian operations. But in the rush to supply peacekeepers, food or shelter, and to measure success in terms of tonnage delivered or lives saved, it is easy to forget that the external intervention predominant during this phase is very transitory. It soon becomes apparent that what is needed for sustainable reconstruction is local knowledge, networks and support. Home-grown reforms build on pre-existing practices fit the real needs of people and engage them in the process. As a result, they are usually more appropriate and more effective than outside intiatives in achieving the desired goals of public administration reform.

Home-grown reforms, which build on pre-existing practices, are usually more appropriate and more effective than outside intiatives in achieving the desired goals of public administration reform

Nonetheless, foreign technical assistance plays a key role in developing public leadership capacity in post-conflict situations. In Uganda, for example, donor-funded projects have helped train parliamentarians and teach leadership skills to members of civil society organizations. In Southern Sudan, the Government is relying on Kenya's assistance to give Arabic-speaking magistrates a crash course in English, which the South has adopted as its official language.

International organizations' modalities of intervention in post-conflict State-building have differed across regions and time. In some cases, international organizations have worked with State governments, as in Sierra Leone and Afghanistan. In other instances, the international community has established international administrations that can assume legislative and executive powers, as in Cambodia, or they have taken over the whole government, as in Kosovo, Timor-Leste and Iraq (Sambanis 2007). The results of international intervention have been mixed, but experience has yielded useful lessons.

Providing appropriate assistance

One key lesson is that external funding and technical assistance must be sequenced and long-term, focusing on developing capacity from the outset so that governments can mobilize resources domestically. Paradoxically, the most aid is available early on, when crisis or post-conflict governments' absorptive capacity is weakest. When governments actually develop capacity, aid often dries up. Therefore, a care-

External funding and technical assistance must be sequenced and long-term, focusing on developing capacity from the outset so that governments can mobilize resources domestically

ful balance must be struck between short- and long-term initiatives. Capacity-building in institutions must begin immediately, but it must be sequenced realistically, acknowledging that reform programmes need to be incremental, ongoing and long-term. External donors also need to strike a balance between the goal of ensuring accountability and the goal of collaborating effectively with other assistance groups.

Donors often try for quick fixes. Such efforts provide only temporary solutions

In terms of leadership capacity development, the role of donors in providing financial support is very important, as both human resources and economic resources are scarce in post-conflict countries. However, donors often try for quick fixes by bringing in international experts, specialized organizations and non-governmental organizations to work in specific sectors such as security and finance. Such efforts provide only temporary solutions. Once foreign aid has been exhausted, donors find that they have built islands of excellence within public administration but with no sustainable capacity to operate over the long term. If building leadership capacity is about equipping present and future leaders to work together for peace and development, then international donors will be more effective if they provide funding to bring in impartial facilitators to help all political factions jointly shape a vision for their country.

Brinkerhoff (2007, p. 6) sums up the importance of close partnership this way: "Local knowledge is essential in order to move beyond standard intervention templates and generic recipes. An understanding of the local context is especially critical for country-led assistance strategies and support to endogenous capacity development. One way in which donors can increase their knowledge of local contexts is to improve their analysis and rapid reconnaissance tools. Several international actors have already invested in such tools. Another approach for donors to increase their contextual knowledge is to make better use of individuals with country-specific knowledge, both prior to intervention and as members of reconstruction efforts on the ground. This can be accomplished through greater incorporation of members of the national diaspora as well as by increasing the participation of local actors earlier in planning and implementation processes".

Another important issue involving foreign donors is the type of capacity development they typically favour in post-conflict situations. An overemphasis on building technical skills to produce quick wins in terms of service delivery may miss the point of the whole reconstruction process, which is to transform mindsets so that governance is perceived not as a zero-sum game but as an act of collaborative problem-solving. Fostering this cognitive transformation and rebuilding trust among factions should therefore go hand in hand with building the technical skills needed to deliver public services and re-establish peace and security.

To transform mindsets, mechanisms for acculturation to public service are of the utmost importance

To transform mindsets, mechanisms for acculturation to public service are of the utmost importance. Both formal training and informal socialization can help new members of an organization internalize the organization's objectives and respect the roles assigned to them. Schools of public administration should be enhanced to better serve this purpose. Other mechanisms can also be set up to transmit the principles and underlying values of public service and to foster a high degree of identification with the institutional role. In the United Kingdom, for example, before aspiring barristers can practice law, they must belong to an Inns of Court, a professional association that provides informal supplementary education and socialization.

There is a tendency to believe that because of the conditions in post-conflict countries—violence, displacement of people, brain drain and diasporas—leadership capacities there are non-existent. In reality, they exist, but not always where expected. Leadership capacities are as likely to be found in ex-combatants or heads of grass-roots women's organizations, for example, as among government officials. Thus a major concern in post-conflict environments is to create appropriate mechanisms for informal leaders to contribute to the process of peace and reconstruction.

This leads to another important issue, which is that international donors usually focus on rebuilding capacities at the national level while neglecting the local levels. Participatory governance can be an effective tool for engaging citizens in post-conflict reconstruction (as discussed in Chapter V), but its implementation varies greatly, depending on local conditions. For example, in societies that are deeply divided by ethnic, religious or other social identities, decentralization has to be managed carefully so as not to exacerbate conflict. However, whether or not decentralization is appropriate in a given setting, it is clear that greater appreciation of local and country-specific conditions could help in involving local leaders more fully in capacity development programmes.

International donors usually focus on rebuilding capacities at the national level while neglecting the local levels

Coordinating assistance

Coordination needs to occur among donors, between donors and governments, and among ministries

Coordination of efforts to provide leadership capacity development is critical. Coordination needs to occur among donors, between donors and governments, and among ministries. The coordination should be undertaken at the horizontal level, but also vertically among central and local structures that provide capacity development for local leaders.

Regional organizations have also increasingly provided support to countries after violent conflict. In 1992, the United Nations Secretary-General's report on "An Agenda for Peace" advocated for regional organizations to play a greater role in peacekeeping operations, given their knowledge of local conditions. The Department of Peacekeeping Operations has recently intensified dialogue with the African Union to increase its role in mediation and peacekeeping in African countries. Likewise, the European Union has assumed greater involvement in internal crises affecting countries in its own neighbourhood. Regional organizations can also help disseminate knowledge about building leadership capacities. They can organize workshops and seminars to share best practices, and they can facilitate meetings among governments that have recovered from conflict and rebuilt their capacities and those that are struggling to do so. Although situations vary greatly even within a specific region, depending on internal social identities, political circumstances and existing capacities, cooperation among neighbouring governments and the sharing of lessons learned can be powerful tools that contribute to leadership capacity development. ◆

5. Lessons learned

- Developing leadership capacities in post-conflict countries is pre-eminently an endogenous process that should take into account pre-existing belief systems and patterns of behavior. Although it is important to build technical and managerial skills, in order to transform conflict into peaceful cohabitation, the first task is to develop trust between leaders of competing factions and among competing factions themselves. Most importantly, the perception of politics as a zero-sum game needs to be transformed into a mindset that emphasizes collaboration and respect for the underlying values and principles of agreed-upon governance institutions

- In addition to the willingness to adopt a new mindset, post-conflict leaders need other key capacities: the ability to unite citizens behind a shared vision for the future; the ability to manage diversity and foster inclusivness; a willingness to nurture future leaders to ensure smooth succession of power; and skill in communicating with the public and managing citizens' expectations for progress.

- A number of tools and strategies can be adopted to promote capacity development, especially to jump-start the process of transforming mindsets. These tools include visioning workshops and simulation games; leadership coaching; staff exchanges and visits; and peer-to-peer learning. All of these are especially helpful in the immediate phase of reconstruction; however focusing on long-term leadership capacity-building is of essence so as to avoid relapses into violent conflict.

- International and regional donors can most effectively assist in capacity-building if they are sensitive to local conditions and tap into local expertise. They can play a valuable role by providing funding and technical assistance that is sequenced over the long term and coordinated with other partners. The focus should be on facilitating home-grown solutions. In the immediate aftermath of conflict, that might mean bringing together opposing factions for constructive dialogue. In the long term, priority should be given to building the competence of local capacity developers, particularly schools of public administration and other institutional programmes that promote acculturation to public service through training and lifelong learning. ▓

Chapter III
Building Effective Public Administration Institutions

Institutions are generally defined as the rules of the game in economic, political and social interactions. Put another way, they equate to the formal (e.g., the constitution and party systems) rules and procedures governing human behavior. In governance, institutions encompass (i) all standard operating procedures of governments, (ii) more overarching structures of State, and (iii) a nation's normative social order (Ikenberry 1988).

Only recently has attention been given to public administration reforms, including civil service reforms, in post-conflict States. International organizations and donors have often focused on elections as the political tool for institution-building and on macroeconomic development as the economic engine of growth. International financial institutions have prescribed the reduction of public sector expenditures, including civil service expenditures (Vandermoortele 2003). Yet it is equally important, if not more so, to play explicit attention to institution-building as an ongoing process in post-conflict societies.[9]

This chapter begins by looking at the key issues involved in building institutions after conflict. It then discusses ways to strengthen public sector institutions, focusing on the civil service, legislative institutions and the judiciary. It also addresses mechanisms to improve the public sector's performance in delivering public services and preventing relapses into conflict.

---

[9] The three priorities in post-conflict institution-building, according to Jolicoeur (2004), are (i) disarmament and the rehabilitation and integration of refugees, (ii) elections and (iii) respect for human rights.

1. Public administration institutions as foundations of good governance

Building or rebuilding governance institutions, whether in a post-conflict context or under less challenging circumstances, is a complex task. When discussing the subject, it helps to keep four points in mind. First, *governance is a broader concept than public administration;* it encompasses public administration but refers more sweepingly to "the exercise of economic, political and administrative authority to manage a country's affairs at all levels" (UNDP 1997).[10] Taking this into account, countries rebuilding their governance systems should guard against focusing only institutions of government. In fact, to ensure sustainable development and peace, it is critical to design governance institutions that promote the collaboration and participation of all stakeholders from all sectors (the public sector, private sector, and civil society).

A second point to remember is that *governance and public administration institutions are purposeful instruments for achieving national political and socio-economic objectives.* Therefore, building such institutions should be viewed not as a value-free, technical re-engineering process that can be outsourced to external actors, but rather as the most significant task for a nation's people in the aftermath of a civil war. The overriding purpose for developing governance and public administration institutions must be to support the development process and meet post-conflict challenges.

Building governance institutions should be viewed not as a value-free re-engineering process, but rather as the most significant task for a nation's people

Third, *every post-conflict situation is unique and requires a unique institutional development strategy, which should begin from an accurate assessment of the past.* The degree of institutional development needed in each country depends on the nature of the systems and institutions, practices and behaviours, and local political culture that were present before the upsurge of violence. Redesigning democratic institutions in countries where they previously existed is very different from designing new governance institutions where there were none before. In addition, institution-building is af-

Every post-conflict situation is unique and requires a unique institutional development strategy

---

[10] Kauzya (2003, p. 1) says, "As an act of steering a people's socio-politico-economic development, governance is a multifaceted compound situation of institutions, systems, structures, processes, procedures, practices, relationships, and leadership behaviour in the exercise of social, political, economic, and managerial / administrative authority in the running of public or private affairs." He adds that "good governance is the exercise of this authority with the participation, interest, and livelihood of the governed as the driving force".

fected by the duration of a conflict and the way it ends (with a negotiated peace settlement, a power-sharing arrangement, or the outright victory of one party).

Fourth, *there is no road map for building institutions that ensure peace and prosperity in post-conflict situations, but there are signposts for effective institutional development and capacity-building.*[11] These include:

- Designing, in a participatory way, a comprehensive national programme for strengthening governance and public administration;
- Developing a shared vision and clear mission for governance and public administration institutions;
- Creating formal frameworks for good governance;
- Harmonizing traditional and modern institutions; and
- Promoting participatory democracy and local governance.

Each of these is discussed in turn below.

Well-designed institutions are meaningless without capable leaders and civil servants to carry out institutional functions

In general, capacity needs to be built at the individual level (expanding the experience, knowledge and technical skills of leaders and civil servants), and at the organizational level (developing structures, systems, rules, norms, policies, etc.). These levels are interdependent: well-designed institutions are meaningless without capable leaders and civil servants to carry out institutional functions, and leaders and civil servants will be ineffectual in the absence of strong institutions that meet people's needs and have broad support. In post-conflict situations, institutional capacity-building/development is particularly challenging because protracted conflict erodes trust and tolerance among different societal and political groups. Agreeing on and designing the most appropriate governance and public administration institutions in countries recovering from violent conflict is difficult by itself; ensuring that all stakeholders and competing groups respect the institutions built can be even more difficult.

It is beyond the purview of this report to indicate what institutional arrangements are best suited for countries emerging from conflict, because, as we have said, there are no blanket solutions. Instead, we focus on what has borne positive results in the past.

---

[11] "Capacity-building" refers to building capacity in situations where there is none (as in post-conflict reconstruction of public administration). "Capacity" is the ability to evaluate and address the crucial questions related to development policy choices and modes of implementation, based on an understanding of the local context and the needs of the people. It encompasses the country's human, scientific, technological, organizational, institutional and resource capabilities (UNDP). "Capacity development" refers to strengthening and fine-tuning existing capacity.

Designing a comprehensive programme to strengthen governance and public administration through dialogue with stakeholders

As mentioned earlier, countries embarking on post-conflict reconstruction must look at the entire spectrum of governance institutions rather than at the narrow realm of public administration. Furthermore, they must adopt an inclusive, consultative approach when articulating a long-term vision and development strategy for the country. It is only by including all societal stakeholders in this process that competing interests can be reconciled and government activities can be aligned with people's needs. The United Nations Conference on Least Developed Countries discussed this issue and came to the following conclusion:

It is only by including all societal stakeholders that competing interests can be reconciled and government activities can be aligned with people's needs

> *Any meaningful public administration effort should emanate from and be an integral part of a nation-wide programme for promoting and strengthening good governance, peace and stability. Despite this, many LDCs [least-developed countries] still use uncoordinated rule application systems and ineffective welfare structures that stifle the private sector and civil society. The development performance in LDCs will not improve if their governments are reluctant to re-examine and redefine the role of public administration and how it relates to private sector, civil society, and global actors—not only in development but also in the delivery of services and maintenance of stability. (United Nations 2001a)*

It is important to ensure coherence and coordination in designing governance and public administration institutions

It is also important to ensure coherence and coordination in designing governance and public administration institutions, since countries that have taken a piecemeal approach to institution-building have found themselves on shaky ground.

Developing a shared vision and clear mission for governance and public administration institutions

One of the most challenging yet vital tasks for a country in the aftermath of civil war is to create a common vision for the future. Aspirations for socio-politico-economic development—and the challenges that stand in the way—should be discussed and agreed in consultation with a cross-section of the population. At the same time, discussions must address how responsibilities will be shared among different stakeholders and what mechanisms will be used to encourage collaboration and participation by all sectors (public, private and civil society). In South Africa, for example, the African National Congress leadership

Discussions must address how responsibilities will be shared among different stakeholders

prepared a White Paper outlining its proposals for transforming the public service, and then invited—and received—extensive public comment. The White Paper proved to be a very effective mechanism for ensuring public participation and achieving unity in the country (Ramsingh 2008).

The first step in strengthening governance and public administration institutions is to specify and agree on their missions and objectives

Therefore, the first step in strengthening governance and public administration institutions is to specify and agree on their missions and objectives and the challenges they are intended to overcome. When this is done with input from all sectors, each stakeholder is more likely to know what the others are doing and how to approach collaboration. There is also a sense of empowerment that derives from being part of the solution, which makes stakeholders less likely to resort to violence in the future.

In laying out a vision for the future, actors in post-conflict situations need to acknowledge the past

In laying out a vision for the future, actors in post-conflict situations need to acknowledge the past. Without this, the forces that led to the conflict may be left unresolved and may resurface again. In addition, it is important to thoroughly analyze current capacities, challenges and opportunities. Finally, plans for the future need to clearly spell out the strategic actions and programmatic activities to be undertaken to reconfigure the State. One important part of this process is to review and restate the missions of the State as they relate to the country's development aspirations.

Creating formal frameworks for governance

Sustainable peace requires legal and constitutional frameworks for governance that must be constructed through a process of inclusive participation, especially if they are expected to be visionary enough to lay the foundation for democratic development. While short-term needs may have to be met through an interim, unilaterally constructed constitution, the rewards of a carefully designed participatory process to build an enduring framework will be worth the time. National and international actors should jointly invest in these efforts. They secure the State's legitimacy, increase its credibility and build commitment to democracy. Although participation may take different forms, it should allow the people to draw on their history, suffering and aspirations to create a constitution truly reflective of their needs and vision.

National constitutions that reflect consensus on national socio-politico-economic interests are critical to the survival of any institutional arrangements that are put in place. Constitutions are also the basic guarantors of the rule of law—"the principle that all persons, institutions and entities, public and private, including the State itself, are accountable to laws that are publicly promulgated, equally enforced and independently adjudicated, and which are consistent with international human rights norms and standards" (United Nations 2004, p. 4).[12]

Early on, rule-of-law reform must promote greater transparency and accountability in public administration agencies that handle things like vehicle registration, building permits, rubbish removal, public health inspection, banking regulations and tax collection, since more people have contact with these agencies (and their history of discriminatory practices and corruption) than they do with the formal judiciary. Any continuing bad practices by government agencies can quickly deepen lawlessness and reinforce the perception that the situation is out of control or has not changed.

Rule-of-law reform must promote greater transparency and accountability in public administration agencies

Inconsistencies in legislation and regulations also undermine the rule of law. Bergling et al. (2008, p. 16) point out that "confusion regarding the applicable law is a serious problem in many post-crisis societies. The problem is often compounded by lack of established traditions, practices and principles. Timor-Leste and Liberia are cases in point. In want of clear laws and norms, individuals here may be subjected to arbitrary treatment and have few means of redress under an extremely weak oversight system. For weak and vulnerable groups, who depend on predictable service delivery, for example in relation to health and medicine, unclear rules or sudden changes in policy and practice can have particularly adverse effects. For other groups such as businessmen, arbitrariness and discretion discourage investment and provide incentives for short-sighted opportunistic behaviour.

Constitutions are most durable and stable when they are made through broad consultation and negotiation

Constitutions can be crafted in a number of ways, depending on the particularities of a given country and the aspirations of its people. However, constitutions are most durable and stable when they are made through broad consultation and negotiation to ensure that all socio-politico-economic forces of the country agree on the rules of the game and put the interests of the people at the center of everything. Unfortunately, in some countries emerging from conflict, the problem is not so much the absence of national constitutions but rather disrespect for their provisions. Constitutions may spell out institutional arrangements and rules on paper, but public officials may disregard these in practice. Therefore,

---

[12] The United Nations system is currently supporting national rule-of-law efforts in 116 countries, including 24 countries emerging from conflict. Recently a new interdepartmental and inter-agency mechanism was established to ensure policy coherence and coordination among these entities.

involving all parties in constitution making or constitutional reforms is particularly critical in post-crisis situations, where conflict can arise from disagreements over the distribution of power among public bodies, or the composition, functions and competencies of these entities.

Aware of numerous failed governments, many countries are now undertaking national efforts to elicit the aspirations of the citizenry, and then following up with arduous constitutional formation and re-formulation processes. Mechanisms for articulating citizens' interests (such as a system of political parties) and for developing a culture of pluralism need to be enshrined in national constitutions, just as checks and balances among different branches of government are. Most importantly, a strong bill of fundamental rights needs to be included, to secure a range of protections for citizens and to impose responsibilities on the government and the public sector. When a constitution contains safeguards against injustices (such as freedom from arbitrary arrest and torture), as well as civil rights (the right to equality), political rights (the right to vote) and economic rights (the right to employment), it impels the government and the public sector to provide an environment for the realization of those rights.

Harmonizing traditional and modern institutions

Post-conflict governments need to find workable ways to accommodate traditional institutions and to define their spheres of authority in various areas

All post-conflict countries have different historical legacies—they have adapted in diverse ways to internal and external pressures, had differing experiences with colonizing powers (where these existed) and developed diverse relationships with new governments after independence. Yet while each country has evolved in a unique way, each has a rich history of traditional leaders and institutions that generally co-exist in an uneasy equilibrium with modern institutions of the State.

Post-conflict governments need to find workable ways to accommodate traditional institutions and to define their spheres of authority in areas such as family, marriage, land and certain criminal and civil matters. There are examples of African countries adapting traditional institutions to the needs of modern public administration with some success. Uganda reintroduced kingdoms and traditional leadership institutions but conferred on them missions related to economic development and cultural development. Rwanda introduced the gacaca court system, based on traditional communal law-enforcement practices, to meet the challenges brought about by the genocide of 1994. It is hoped that the gacaca courts, which are well understood by the common man and woman, will not only enable the State to expedite the handling of some genocide-related cases but also facilitate reconciliation at the grass-roots level.

Promoting participatory democracy and local governance

This chapter has already touched on the need for broad public engagement in various aspects of post-conflict reconstruction. Over the past years there has been growing consensus that no single actor—private or public—has the capacity to solve on its own the complex and diversified problems that post-conflict societies confront. Partnerships between the State, the private sector and civil society institutions have proven to be very important in both social service delivery and policymaking in such areas as the protection of the environment, work conditions, and social safety nets. Such success is predicated on building and maintaining an institutional framework open to diversity and hospitable to stakeholders' involvement in policymaking and evaluation processes. Although this is not always easy, evidence has shown that success in modern government depends largely on widening citizen participation and galvanizing support for broadly shared objectives. Recognizing this, the Charter of the Public Service in Africa includes the following statement in article 9:

> *It shall be the responsibility of the administration to ensure that the mechanisms of participation and consultation involving civil society and other stakeholders are effectively put in place through consultative forums and advisory bodies.*

However, one of the problems confronting countries emerging from years of violent conflict is how to create structures that promote and support the participation of the people in determining the direction and content of their socio-politico-economic development. Many countries may be ready to introduce participatory democracy, but the issue of how to do so is still unsettled.

One measure being used by some countries is decentralization, which has the effect of strengthening local councils and other organizations that give local actors a voice in public affairs. Whether decentralization is explicitly implemented or occuring de facto, it is empowering local populations to participate in planning and managing their development. Chapter V provides a more comprehensive picture of decentralization and other mechanisms for encouraging broad participation in post-conflict public administration reconstruction. ◆

Institutional capacity and competencies must be developed in the management and operation of national democratic institutions, including national assemblies, the judiciary and the executive

The civil service should be based on the accepted principles of neutrality, legality and continuity

2. Strengthening public sector institutions

During protracted civil strife, a country's institutional and organizational structures tend to succumb to decay and neglect. In most cases, a government that comes after conflict finds the inherited institutions inadequate to the challenges of the new era. In post-apartheid South Africa, the public service institutions and structures had to be dismantled and drastically restructured to cope with new demands and meet the growing expectations of previously marginalized demographic groups. In Uganda, the autocratic public service inherited from the Amin and Obote regimes had to be completely overhauled in line with the policy of the National Resistance Movement.

Systems and structures need to be devised and implemented based not only on the ways that government ministries are differentiated but also on the ways they work together

The institutional and structural arrangement of the public service will be determined by the missions and objectives it takes on and the way it defines its relations with the public. Realistically, the natural tendency is to fall back to the traditional design of the bureaucratic public service. However, a post-conflict government that is genuinely concerned with avoiding the mistakes of the past (the mistakes that led to the conflict in the first place) will avoid returning to the status quo. The questions involved in rebuilding the public service—what new institutions; what new structures; what new laws, rules and regulations; and what new systems, processes and procedures should be put in place—need to be addressed through a consultative process that may be painful and will certainly require patience and technical know-how. The difficulty is that patience and technical know-how are often lacking in post-conflict or crisis situations. Institutional capacity and competencies must be developed in the management and operation of national democratic institutions, including national assemblies, the judiciary and the executive.

The civil service

One of the institutions that operationalizes and sustains State action is the civil service. Governments all over the world have historically engaged in efforts to make their civil service institutions effective. Countries emerging from conflict cannot be an exception to this. The civil service should be based on the accepted principles of neutrality, legality and continuity, as well as the fundamental values of professionalism, ethics, integrity and moral rectitude. The civil service is especially critical to the development process since it is at the center of planning, implementing, monitoring and evaluating the delivery of essential public services (health care, education, agricultural extension, environmental protection, etc.) that are vital for reducing poverty. Countries that do not have effective civil service institutions are likely to lag behind in achievement of the Millennium Development Goals.

The civil service is an institution composed of sub-institutions. Therefore, developing its capacity may depend on determining which sub-institutions need to be strengthened in which ways. Some institutions are responsible for coordination, others are responsible for control, and yet others are operational. Systems and structures need to be devised and implemented based not only on the ways that government ministries are differentiated but also on the ways they work together. It is difficult to prescribe one way of organizing government ministries. However, it is worth noting that some post-conflict countries have set up separate ministries of information and technology to handle the technological retooling so vital to reconstruction (improving Internet connectivity, establishing computer-based information networks such as LANS and WANS, etc.). By not relegating this work to the Ministry of Communications or another body, these countries are making a strong commitment to technological capacity-building.

Historically, external funding for public administration reform has been much lower than funding for economic liberalization and growth, including privatizations and other economic policy planning and advice. In Guatemala, Tajikistan and Sierra Leone, donors pledged and gave much more financial support to enterprise and economic development than to the reform of public administration (Nakaya 2009). Therefore, to rebuild and revive the institutional structure in post-conflict countries, private consultancy can be used, or a more home-grown approach can be preferred. In Uganda, for instance, the reform of public service was assigned to the Public Service Review and Reorganization Committee, which designed a programme supervised by the Ministry of Public Service. The programme limited the number of cabinet ministries to 22, which put an end to the previous problem of proliferation of ministries. This measure also contributed to the containment of the patronage-based spoils system, making room for more effective, transparent and accountable organizational structures in public administration (Katorobo 2007).

Historically, external funding for public administration reform has been much lower than funding for economic liberalization and growth

Success in public administration reform in post-conflict situations depends much on the will to combat corruption

The Government of Rwanda, on the other hand, hired a consultancy firm based in Boston to assist the country in drafting its public administration reform strategy. This approach was also relatively successful, because as in the Ugandan case, the formalization of the reforms succeeded a long gestation period when inclusive brainstorming on the possible restructuring took place (Katorobo 2007).

The successful institutionalization of a new public administration system with a reformed civil service in post-conflict countries hinges upon the new government's approach to corruption. Several post-conflict States have introduced new institutions to break the chains of corrupt dealings in governance. Uganda and Rwanda have created the office of Inspector General of Government, modeled after the Scandinavian institution of the Ombudsman. The office of the Auditor General, which ensures financial accountability, is a complementary institution. In Uganda, the Auditor General's reports are scrutinized by parliamentary fiscal accountability committees (Katorobo 2007).

Uganda also has a Ministry of Ethics and Transparency, which is responsible for the overall implications of new laws and policies with regard to corruption. An independent agency specializing in the control and monitoring of public tendering and procurement was also put in place. The successful anti-corruption institutions in Uganda suggest the benefit of several specialized institutions dealing with sectors susceptible to corruption, rather than a big umbrella institution watching all corruption matters.

Like Uganda, Nepal has also institutionalized an anti-corruption focus in its post-conflict reconstruction. It has created a separate department, the Special Police Department, to prevent corruption, and the Commission for Investigation of Abuse of Authority (CIAA) to curb corrupt practices among public officials, including the Prime Minister and other government representatives. Under the CIAA, a specialized group called the Property Investigation Judicial Commission has been empowered to deal specifically with the cases of retired civil servants and ex-ministers. Special courts were also established to deal exclusively with corruption cases filed by the CIAA. In addition, Nepal, like Uganda, has a separate commission that deals with financial irregularities (Roshi 2008).

Giving explicit attention to human capacity development and management in the public service, heeding the increasingly important role of information and communication technologies in successful public administration, and opting for inclusive and gradual processes of public administration reform have been some of the hallmarks of post-conflict institution-building. In all three of these areas, civil service reform has been undertaken as a precursor to successful policy-making in development and governance. Some of the focal points for reform have been (i) the statutory basis underlying civil servants' rights and duties, (ii) the relation of employment categories and grades to salary structures and benefits, and (iii) procedures for recruitment, promotion, disciplinary action and termination.

The case of the civil service in Cambodia illustrates that all these points must be addressed holistically if public administration reform is to succeed. The Cambodian civil service suffered from ineffective deployment of inadequate numbers of personnel in needed areas such as health care and education. Many civil servants had little education, and salaries were so low that most held secondary jobs as an additional source of revenue. Frequent absenteeism resulted, and corruption soared as well, partly because of the low pay and partly because of inflexible and constraining staff categorization, automatic promotion based on time spent in the service rather than performance, and weak incentives for career development. Because civil service reform in Cambodia addressed all of these issues holistically rather than piecemeal, it has constituted the stepping-stone to comprehensive public administration reform.

In order to foster a new relationship between civil servants and citizens, public sector institutions ought to incorporate mechanisms that allow for openness, flexibility in the face of change, and, most importantly, accountability to the public at large. Greater attention is being given to developing a more service-oriented spirit among civil servants and to ensuring effective and transparent mechanisms for citizens to voice complaints concerning poor-quality, inefficient or inaccessible public services. Flexible structures and processes are being favoured over the more traditional and bureaucratic patterns. This is important because the ability of governments to "include and synergize", as well as "listen and respond", are almost universally accepted as an important source of policy legitimation" (United Nations 2001b).

To foster a new relationship between civil servants and citizens, public sector institutions ought to incorporate mechanisms that allow for openness, flexibility in the face of change, and accountability to the public at large

Legislative institutions

The functions of the legislature include representation of the people, law-making and oversight of the executive. For this reason, the legislature is a critical institution in representative democracy, defending the

Experience shows that in many countries, the legislature has suffered under overbearing executives and their coercive wing, the military

interests of citizens, making just laws to provide a basis for the rule of law and ensuring accountability of the executive, especially for the way it deploys public resources, power and authority. Experience shows that in many countries, the legislature has suffered under overbearing executives and their coercive wing, the military. Therefore, one of the institutions that requires revamping and strengthening in post-conflict environments is the legislature. Measures that could be taken to strengthen legislatures include the following:

- Creating national constitutions that specify the legislature's structure and functions and provide it with adequate power, authority and constitutional legitimacy to control the excesses of the executive;
- Establishing good working methods for Parliament and its sub-units, with respect to management of time, the legislative agenda and disciplinary rules;
- Enhancing the legislative and management skills of legislatures and their aides, including skills in drafting legislation, conducting investigations for committee work and handling the budget and budgetary process;
- Structuring or restructuring the organizational set-up of parliamentary committees and improving their effectiveness by building capacities for process skills such as negotiation and mediation;
- Developing greater public awareness of the legislature's work and significance by, for example, broadcasting parliamentary sessions on national radio and television, keeping most legislative and committee sessions open to the public and engaging in formal and informal education about the role of the legislative branch;
- Strengthening legislators' outreach to and communication with their constituencies by establishing local, staffed constituency offices, using communications technologies for conveying opinions, and encouraging legislators to hold or attend town meetings in their districts and participate in other forums.
- Linking national legislatures to local legislatures so that there is no contradiction between the legislatures at these different levels.

The judiciary

Reforms aimed at building an independent and effective judiciary are critical to ensuring the rule of law, protecting life and property, building a working system of checks and balances to guarantee fundamental rights, and solving disputes among different levels of government as well as various socio-politico-economic actors. In addition, an independent and competent judiciary is necessary for promoting both local and foreign investment. One of the factors contributing to the inability of post-conflict countries to attract investment is the inadequacy of judicial systems to provide predictable dispute-resolution mechanisms through which investors can be assured of the security of their investments.

Reforming the judiciary is, however, a complex task that goes beyond the mere act of redesigning judicial institutions

Reforming the judiciary is, however, a complex task that goes beyond the mere act of redesigning judicial institutions. The case of Sub-Saharan Africa offers an interesting example and useful lessons on why institutional reforms are quite difficult to implement. As pointed out in the Introduction, several Sub-Saharan countries have experienced internal conflict over the past decades. They all had judicial systems in place before violence broke out, yet these systems were unable to facilitate peaceful resolutions of festering disputes. A closer look at the judicial systems of these countries will provide an explanation for their failure.

The main feature of Sub-Saharan countries' judicial systems is that they were all imported. That is to say, they were models transplanted from Western countries by European colonial authorities and placed in "alien" contexts. The Gambia, Nigeria, Sierra Leone, Uganda and Liberia have common law systems (Liberia's is based on American common law; the other countries follow English common law). Cameroon is peculiar in that the north has adopted a French civil law system while the south has a common law system. Namibia and South Africa have a Roman-Dutch civil system. Somalia has an Italian version of the civil law system, although many of its clans are resorting to the Islamic Sharia form of justice. These judicial systems did not operate while civil war was ongoing, but they now have been or are being re-established in all countries except Somalia.

Judicial systems, like other institutions, embody both formal rules and embedded belief systems and values. Because the civil law (or inquisitorial) system and the common law (accusatorial) system evolved in different historical contexts,[13] they reflect two different conceptions of the State's function. Whereas the inquisitorial system is a feature of strongly centralized States in which the government manages the lives

Judicial systems, like other institutions, embody both formal rules and embedded belief systems and values

---

[13] The inquisitorial system developed in continental Europe during the absolutist era as an instrument of the king's centralizing efforts. By contrast, in the Anglo-Saxon world, where absolutism failed to take hold, the old forms of mediation, which were more accusatorially based, prevailed and justice remained a prerogative of the community, which was represented by justices of the peace or jurors.

of people, the adversarial system is the product of a liberal type of State in which government maintains the social equilibrium and provides a framework for social self-management. Where government is conceived of as a manager, the administration of justice seems to be directed towards the implementation of State policies, whereas where government maintains the social equilibrium, the administration of justice tends to be associated with conflict resolution (Damaska 1986). In inquisitorial systems, the high degree of faith in the State and its institutions that allows the entire case to be entrusted to "non-partisan" State-officials is unthinkable without the underlying ideological assumptions about the individual's relationship to the State and society, and about the best way of serving the public interest.

The choice of judicial models should reflect the way political power is structured and particularly the role of the State vis à-vis society

Such differences, which go far beyond mere technicalities, were not carefully taken into consideration when transferring specific judicial systems to certain developing countries and war-torn societies. The adoption of these models was not consistent with the way political power is structured and particularly with the role of the State vis-à-vis society.

In Sub-Saharan Africa, for example, as in most traditional societies, the tendency is to resolve conflicts through forms of mediation such as negotiation, conciliation and arbitration. The traditional arbitration procedure is simple, transparent and shorn of the legalisms associated with "foreign" law. The contending parties typically present their cases in front of third parties who have been chosen by the community based on their social standing, their reputation for fairness and their oratorical skills, including ability to sum up evidence with proverbs and idioms. The arbitrators' task is to direct the oral debate, allow comments and interjections from other bystanders and, after weighing the submissions, decide how blame and credit should be fairly shared by the plaintiffs and the respondents. It is rare for one side to walk away with absolute victory while the other is pronounced totally at fault. The ultimate goal of justice is to reconcile the interests at stake so as to re-establish social order and ensure the stability of social relations. The judicial process thus favours compromise, perceiving it as a device to recompose and strengthen solidarity among the members of society. This stems in part from a traditional vision of social life and organization in which individuals see themselves as community members first and foremost, and place the community's integrity and cohesion above the redress of wrongs to individuals (Alberti 1997).

This view of how society should function and how disputes should be solved was clearly not taken into account when Western judicial institutions were first imported to African countries. Not surprisingly, then, the legitimacy of these institutions was always in question. When formal judicial institutions do not serve their intended purpose and are not perceived as legitimate, contending parties may prefer to seek justice within parallel, pre-existing mediation structures. Even worse, parties may not accept as binding the decisions taken by formal courts of law. Legal decisions may actually aggravate rather than settle the tensions among different parts of society, and the law may be seen as destructive of the established order rather than as a means to keep the peace.

Thus, introducing sophisticated rules and procedures to govern conflict resolution will not by itself forestall violence if the rules are not perceived by "users" as legitimate. Because consent is at the basis of a working system of justice, judicial systems should not be imposed from above but instead adapted and integrated into the legal environment in which they are to operate.

Introducing sophisticated rules and procedures to govern conflict resolution will not by itself forestall violence if the rules are not perceived by "users" as legitimate

In enacting judicial reforms in post-conflict situations, the processes and practices of the judiciary need to be made relevant to current conditions, and the system needs to be made understandable and accessible to all, including the poor. The following measures are also recommended to strengthen the judiciary:

- Specific procedures should be clearly defined for the training, recruitment and advancement of all judges and court officials, to protect the judiciary from interference by political bodies or contending parties. In general, the keys to an independent judiciary include long-term appointments or lifetime tenure, merit-based promotions, adequate salaries and status parity with other government officials.
- Improvements should be made to the operation and working modalities of the judicial system. For example, mediation and arbitration techniques can be introduced as alternatives to going to court to resolve disputes.
- A code of ethics should be spelled out, along with plans for implementing it, imposing sanctions and raising awareness among both the judicial community and the public.
- Effort should be made to ensure a satisfactory working environment, adequate infrastructure and adequate building facilities.

- Information and communication technologies should be used to facilitate working modalities and internal operations, especially concerning records.
- Competent and corruption-free commercial courts should be established to settle business disputes expeditiously.
- In the current context of globalization and regional integration, judicial systems and institutions should be cognizant of international legal frameworks, international laws and international dispute resolution mechanisms. ◆

3. Improving public sector performance

Building effective mechanisms for citizen-centric public service delivery

Post-conflict recovery will not be sustainable unless governments, civil society and other stakeholders acquire the capacities and skills to manage and resolve conflict

The provision of efficient and affordable public services for all, including vulnerable groups and minorities, is one of the core functions of the State and a key to reducing poverty. It is also crucial to ensuring widespread support for the government and, more specifically, public administration institutions. Therefore, it is imperative to develop new and more efficient tools for improving the delivery of services, including performance and monitoring systems, client surveys, and effective outsourcing mechanisms. In this respect, one of the greatest challenges is identifying which services can be more effectively provided by the market and which, instead, should be the sole responsibility of the public sector. Improving the delivery of services, their quality and their social impact requires (i) enhanced leadership capacity, as discussed in Chapter II; (ii) changes in the organizational structure and culture of the public sector and (iii) policies for human resources development, as discussed in Chapter IV.

Building an infrastructure for peace

Some observers believe that post-conflict recovery will not be sustainable unless governments, civil society and other stakeholders acquire the capacities and skills to manage and resolve, through compromise and consensus, recurring conflicts over scarce resources, the allocation of mineral wealth, land or identity. While many recovery efforts focus on the rebuilding of physical infrastructure, equal emphasis must be placed on building an "infrastructure for peace"—the institutions and processes through which a society anticipates and mediates its conflicts.

The United Nations Millennium Declaration, in addressing issues of peace and security, highlights not only short-term conflict prevention, but also long-term governance and development. This is because most of the violent conflicts that have rocked the world and hindered development are a consequence of failures in governance and public administration systems. While efforts must be made to stop violence where it has erupted, governance and administration institutions should have the requisite institutional and human capacities to foresee possible sources of violent conflict and try to avert them. The capacities of community, national, regional, and international institutions should be strengthened to analyze policy and distributive issues with a view to avoiding violence.

Institutions of governance contribute to stability and peace by creating platforms for resolving disputes, sharing perspectives and balancing competing societal interests. The separation of powers among three branches of government, each responsible for serving the public in different ways, provides multiple access points for citizen involvement and platforms for resolving differences. The greater the number, diversity and effectiveness of these platforms, at both national and local levels, the greater the possibility of peaceful resolution of disputes. The more regular and frequent the interactions among diverse elements in society, the greater the potential for sustainable security and peace. Consequently, institutional structures need to be designed and strengthened so they can facilitate ongoing interaction among different development stakeholders.

The disputes that trigger violence generally involve policy decisions over the distribution of resources, political power or territorial boundaries. Preventing the eruption of destructive conflict depends largely on the degree to which national and local leaders and governance institutions can manage tensions among different ethnic groups, religious groups or marginalized parties. The goal of conflict prevention is not to eradicate conflict per se, but rather to manage conflict situations so that they don't escalate into violence, repression, institutional maladministration or structural injustice. Effective management of conflict aims further than preventing or limiting the negative consequences of violence, exclusion or disaffection. It aims to generate positive outcomes from the synergy of airing competing viewpoints, building consensus around divi-

Post-conflict countries should build an "infrastructure for peace"—the institutions and processes through which a society anticipates and mediates its conflicts

Infusing conflict analysis and management techniques into internal, as well as external governance practices is key to avoiding conflict relapses

sive issues, solving problems jointly and, ultimately, transforming antagonistic relationships into respectful, tolerant ones that can enable communities to develop peacefully and sustainably.

Conflict management constitutes an essential part of the everyday work of all governments, whether the country is approaching or in the midst of violent crisis, recovering from conflict, or in a stable, non-violent situation. Infusing conflict analysis and management techniques into internal, as well as external, governance practices can help government administrators improve decision-making and coordination among ministries, resolve policy issues between branches of government, and smooth out implementation problems among tiers of government and with civil society. Improving conflict management skills will also help government officials to communicate and manage negotiate more effectively with civil society, organized labor and the private sector, as well as with bilateral donors and intergovernmental agencies.

A two-pronged approach should be taken. First, special emphasis should be placed on strengthening conflict-mitigating institutions such as ombudsman institutions, minority commissions, national and local mediation centers, human rights offices, contemporary and traditional judicial systems, alternative dispute resolution systems and the educational institutions that train personnel for all of the above. Secondarily, conflict management skills and sensitivity need to be infused broadly into the policies and programmes of all government offices to deal with internal policy and procedures as well as facilitate their interface with the public.

Particular emphasis should be placed on developing conflict-mitigating institutions

In sum, a combination of factors determines whether institutions in post-conflict situations are sustainable and likely to head off the recurrence of violence. These factors include:

- The degree of consensus on the institutions' underlying values and purpose;
- The level of political commitment by leaders and followers to adhere to the values and purpose of the newly established institutions;
- The extent to which the institutions (including their purposes, operating structures and rules) are perceived as legitimate and deserving of allegiance and trust;
- The modernity-tradition ratio—that is, the balance struck between the need for continuity and the need for change within the institutions;

- The institutions' capacity to manage diversity and prevent conflict;
- The dependability of theconflict resolution mechanisms and;
- The capacity of actors to perform according to institutional rules. (Alberti and Balogun, 2005) ◆

4. Lessons learned

- Rebuilding appropriate governance and public administration institutions is critical for ensuring peace and security, human rights and socio-economic development in countries emerging from violent conflict.
- Developing mechanisms to ensure that political and administrative actors behave according to agreed-upon institutional rules and values is critical in securing a high degree of institutionalization.
- Post-conflict situations are heterogeneous, and therefore there are no "one size fits all" institutional solutions to governance challenges. In each country, institutional reforms should be tailored to current needs while taking into acount the legacy of pre-existing institutions, including past values and belief systems. Rebuilding the same institutions that led to violent conflict should be avoided, but some traditional practices might be worthy of retaining or creatively adapting.
- Institutional reforms should be negotiated among all stakeholders and should appear to solve concrete challenges. Genuine inclusion of all parties in the reconstruction of governance and public administration is the foundation for long-lasting peace and development. In addition, for a particular institutional reform to be accepted and embraced within the public sector, it must be seen as adding value by helping to solve a problem. It should respond to a felt need by stakeholders who agree on a common definition of the problem.
- Institutional reforms are more sustainable when change arises from within the country, or when internal leaders collaborate intensely with external actors, rather than when reforms are imposed from the outside.

- Successfully adopting new institutional models depends not only on designing the formal rules, but also on understanding the values and belief systems underlying those institutions.
- Post-conflict public administration institutions must be well-designed, but it is equally important for the rules and expected behaviours they embody to be internalized by leaders and all other actors.
- Building an infrastructure for peace, including institutions and mechanisms to mediate disputes, is critical in preventing a relapse into conflict. ■

Chapter IV

Strengthening Human Resources in the Public Service

The public service is integral to the social, political, economic and cultural life of every country. Consequently, in conflict situations, the public service is generally both a contributing factor to the conflict and a casualty of it. It is also a central actor in the reconstruction process, and as such, the public service must transform itself so that it can appropriately manage the changed and changing public administration environment.

This chapter looks first at why a strong public service is so important in post-conflict situations, and how human resources capacity varies from country to country. The chapter then focuses on challenges and strategies related to the development of human resources capacity after conflict. It addresses the following issues: controlling the number of public servants on the payroll; practicing merit-based recruitment; promoting transparency, accountability, integrity, professionalism and ethics; respecting diversity in the public service and tapping its potential benefits; paying civil servants in a post-conflict situation; and counteracting brain drain.

1. The central role of the public service

The success of government in a post-conflict society depends on the performance of the public service in providing critical services to the population and restoring trust and confidence in governance. This is because the public service constitutes the heartbeat of any government. Public servants pervade the entire sphere of government action. They are schoolteachers delivering education services; they are medical practitioners (doctors, nurses, midwives, public health workers, etc.) providing a whole range of health services; they are judges and other court personnel handling judicial matters; they are police officers keeping law and order; they are military men and women ensuring security; they are agricultural extension workers, road constructors, forestry officers, administrative officials, parliamentarians, finance officers, planners, etc. Not only are public servants engaged in every facet of government activity, but most of them work directly with citizens, to whom they represent the face of government. Therefore, the quality of public servants in terms of knowledge, skills, attitudes and networks can make or break public trust in a post-conflict government.

"Trust in government" may refer to people's faith that the institutions of government are working well and predictably. It may mean trusting that government employees are competent and ethical. It may also be a matter of appreciating government services and viewing them as equitably provided. However trust in government is defined, the role of human resources is paramount. The challenges facing post-conflict countries can be adequately addressed only by competent and committed public servants. Yet in most post-conflict cases, the public service has become dysfunctional or altogether destroyed. Therefore, a priority for post-conflict reconstruction is to build the capacities of public administration personnel. Strengthening public servants' knowledge, skills, networks and attitudes is key to any improvement in government performance, because it is through public servants that services are planned and delivered, critical innovations conceived and realized, needed reforms carried out and trust in government restored. ◆

Strengthening public servants' knowledge, skills, networks and attitudes is key to any improvement in government performance, because it is through public servants that services are planned and delivered

2. Variation in human resources capacity after conflict

Rebuilding human capacities in the public service should proceed from an accurate assessment of the past since post-conflict public administration situations are not always similar

Post-conflict public administration situations are not always similar. Human capacities in the public service break down in different ways, depending on the nature of the conflict and the conditions that obtain afterward. Consequently, countries will face different challenges in rebuilding their human resources capabilities, and experience gained in one situation may not be relevant in another. For example, in South Africa after the fall of the apartheid regime, the institutions, systems, structures and even personnel of the public service were in place and intact. But they were all suited to the apartheid regime, which needed to be dismantled and replaced by a people-oriented, representative public service. According to Ramsingh (2008), the employee profile of the Public Service did not reflect the demographics of the South African society, as members of the privileged white minority were grossly overrepresented and occupied key positions. There was no equity in the employment conditions of public servants, as these were largely determined along racial lines, with the white minority receiving the most favorable benefits. The public service was shrouded in secrecy and corrupt practices, with little to no emphasis on accountability and transparency.

The South African situation was different from the one in Rwanda after the 1994 genocide, when most public servants were killed. Most of the rest, particularly those implicated in genocidal acts, escaped into Zaire (now the Democratic Republic of Congo) carrying files, records and other movable public service assets. When these exiles returned to Rwanda, they took over public offices in an unauthorized, uncoordinated manner. This "created a major problem for the incoming administration, especially, that of how to eject the new self-declared officials and ensure that vacancies were filled in an orderly fashion" (Katorobo 2007, p. 55). By the time the new regime settled in, knowledgeable and skilled personnel were unavailable, and the public service's systems and institutions, along with equipment, office space and logistics, were severely lacking.

A somewhat similar situation existed in Timor-Leste after 1999. An estimated 7,000 Indonesian civil servants had fled the Territory after Indonesian rule collapsed, and institutions and public records were destroyed or removed. This left a vacuum in all areas of government, because Indonesian officials had formerly occupied most of the technical positions, as well as senior and middle management positions, and there had been limited development of Timorese skills in administration and governance. Furthermore, whereas some of the Rwandans who returned after the genocide were eager to work and reconstruct their country, the Indonesians who fled Timor-Leste had little interest in returning. When the United Nations took over the administration of the Territory, there was no such thing as the Timor-Leste public service. Initially the United Nations had to rely on Member State volunteers, as new Timorese civil servants were being trained.

Uganda had a very different problem after the civil war that ended in 1986. Uganda's post-conflict public service was overstaffed—bloated by redundant positions with overlapping functions. The system was also plagued by poor remuneration, moonlighting, extensive corruption and uncommitted personnel (Langseth and Mugaju 1996).

These examples illustrate the wide variation in human resource capacity in post-conflict countries. Not surprisingly, then, approaches to strengthening human resources within the public service will vary from country to country. Where a substantial number of personnel have been inherited from the outgoing regime, the task may be simply to change employees' attitudes towards the new government and towards serving the public. Such was the case in Uganda after 1986. In situations such as Rwanda, where the public service has been flooded by returning exiles without the necessary education, skills or experience, then massive immediate retraining is required, not only to transmit knowledge and skills but also to cultivate a sense of togetherness and a shared work ethic. In a situation like Timor-Leste or Kosovo, where United Nations personnel from different countries and cultures constituted an interim public service, the initial concern is to help everyone work together harmoniously in a new environment that is often insecure. ◆

Given the wide variation in human resource capacity in post-conflict countries, approaches to strengthening human resources within the public service should be tailored to local needs

3. Challenges and strategies involved in managing public service personnel

In post-conflict situations where there has been severe disruption or destruction of the public service, every aspect of managing the system's human resources becomes problematic. Recruitment, remuneration,

In many post-conflict situations, one challenge is determining how many public servants are on the government payroll

discipline, promotion, supervision, performance evaluation—these all present challenges. Many factors can lead to poor management of public service personnel, including a lack of employment policies, unclear policies, the absence or breakdown of personnel control systems (including destroyed records), unprofessional employment practices (including politicization, favoritism, tribalism and other forms of patronage), corruption, abuse of power, lack of discipline and so on.

Controlling the number of public servants on the payroll

In many post-conflict situations, one challenge is determining how many public servants are on the government payroll. Getting an exact count of employees is often one of the demands of donors who were funding the post-conflict government, as was the case in Sierra Leone in 2001 (Ulreich 2001). For donors and government leaders, establishing a baseline number of public servants can facilitate planning, restructuring and cost-cutting. Accordingly, they undertake exercises variously referred to as censuses, enumerations, headcounts, staff audits, payroll verifications, or payroll reconciliations. Oftentimes, the work is actually done by foreign consultants, because after destructive conflict, the country may have not enough qualified personnel to take on the task.

Surveys of international experience suggest that enumeration exercises have yielded mixed results. In some cases, they have temporarily eliminated ghost workers, resulting in some savings. For example, in Sierra Leone in 2001, a census of public servants resulted in 6,181 staff being cut from the payroll, saving the country about US$300,000 a month. However, because post-conflict countries generally lack the resources to continue monitoring the number of public service employees. ghost workers are likely to return to the payroll. One of the ironies of post-conflict public administration reconstruction is that on one hand, countries in such situations find that they do not have enough staff to run the public service. On the other hand, a simple tally of workers on the payroll reveals that the number is already more than the country's budget can support.

Several points should be kept in mind here. One is that it is indeed desirable in a post-conflict situation to know precisely how many public servants the country has as it begins reconstructing its public administration capacity. However, the personnel profile should include more than numbers; data should also be gathered about qualifications and skills. The second point is that censuses are very expensive exercises. Therefore they should be planned strategically to fit with the overall objectives for human resources in the public service, especially plans for long-term investment in basic personnel and payroll systems. Third, to be useful, censuses should be designed with the local context in mind, to ensure that the information collected is compatible with the capacity of local staff to analyze it, verify it and use it effectively in a timely manner. Finally, censuses need to be part of a nationally coordinated action with top-level leadership support and local ownership, especially in their design and delivery.

Practicing merit-based recruitment

In most post-conflict situations, recruitment for government positions is poorly controlled, and the civil service quickly grows too large to be effective. Careful steps must be taken to reduce its size without increasing unemployment or creating political problems. If uncontrolled recruitment is not replaced by merit-based recruitment, the public service can continue to fuel conflict, especially over the resources it controls.

When there are already too many people on the payroll, recruiting needed staff constitutes a paradoxical challenge for post-conflict countries. A number of dilemmas arise: What should be done with the existing personnel? Where will people with the right knowledge, skills and attitudes be found? In a situation of broken-down systems, by whom and through what procedures can recruitment be rightly done? How should the politically sensitive issue of layoffs be addressed? To what extent can recruitment be based on merit, given the political compromises that characterize post-conflict situations?

It is always desirable for personnel policy and the recruitment process to be overseen by independent bodies such as civil service commissions, to avoid cronyism, nepotism and favoritism. However, creating and developing such institutions takes time, and in post-conflict situations there is an immediate need to recruit competent personnel. Interim measures to promote merit-based recruitment should therefore be introduced as soon as possible. The earlier this happens, the greater the chances of limiting nepotism, patronage, tribalism and other practices that are harmful to the functioning of the public service.

It is always desirable for personnel policy and the recruitment process to be overseen by independent bodies such as civil service commissions, to avoid cronyism, nepotism and favoritism

In Rwanda in the first few years after the conflict, ministries were allocated to political parties (per the Arusha Accords), and ministerial posts—especially at the lowest levels—were being filled by party members without the requisite qualifications or any public service experience. Since the ministry responsible for the public service was itself allocated to a party, recruitment became a political and controversial issue. In order to make the process objective, a Canadian firm was hired to review applications and conduct interviews, and short-listed candidates had to be vetted by Parliament (Katorobo 2007). Eventually, in 2002, Rwanda established by law the Public Service Commission[14] with a mandate that includes maintaining objectivity and neutrality in the recruitment and management of human resources, and respecting discipline and professional ethics. The Commission is also mandated to organize tests for various positions in the public service and to publish their results.

Promoting transparency, accountability, integrity, professionalism and ethics

Another challenge in reconstructing human resources in the public service after conflict is modifying the behaviour of public servants. In all cases, violence not only thins the ranks of the civil service, but also warps the behaviour and motivation of those who remain. In Bosnia and Herzegovina, for example, the civil servants employed before the war were better educated, better trained and more efficient than their successors in the 1990s and early 2000s. Raised in peacetime and schooled in a comparatively advanced education system, they learned to protect and promote the common good, and they managed government affairs in a relatively effective, rational and efficient manner. The war was the beginning of totally unacceptable behaviour in the public sector. The political parties in power protected certain ethnic and religious interests, and corruption and nepotism flourished (Finca 2007).

Governments should establish institutions, systems and procedures for ensuring transparency and accountability that have been ruptured by the conflict

Post-conflict and crisis situations are known to be breeding grounds for misconduct by public officials. Sometimes this is because institutions, systems and procedures for ensuring transparency and accountability have been ruptured by the conflict. Oftentimes transparency and accountability are overlooked in the rush to handle emergencies and humanitarian relief. But often the problem is that stress and duress trigger the baser instincts in humans, and public servants who would otherwise act ethically succumb to the temptation to use their offices for personal gain. After the conflict ends, such abuse of power remains an acquired habit that is difficult to change.

---

[14] It was not until May 2008, however, that the Public Service Commission was actually constituted.

Another challenge for post-conflict governments is that the public is impatient to see tangible political, economic and social progress. To address citizens' expectations and gain their trust and respect, the government's best strategy is regular and transparent communication with the public. Often, however, systems for sharing information are not in place. Furthermore, to restore confidence in government , the most acute need is for integrity, ethics and professional conduct in the public service. Thus although systems of information dissemination must be designed and implemented, the first priority should be instituting rules, regulations and codes of conduct to guide the behaviour of public servants. In addition, recruitment, induction, and supervision of public servants must be done carefully so that only individuals with strong morals, a strong work ethic and professionalism are hired and retained. This is partly why many post-conflict countries endeavour to establish public service commissions.

Recruitment, induction, and supervision of public servants must be done carefully so that only individuals with strong morals, a strong work ethic and professionalism are hired and retained

Finally, while governments often identify and address the skills gaps and knowledge gaps of public servants, there is often no parallel effort to address the work attitudes and behaviours that maximize or undermine employees' performance. Therefore, another important strategy for post-conflict countries is to incorporate character considerations into employee reviews, professional development programmes, and other performance management systems.

Respecting diversity and tapping its potential benefits

In most post-conflict and crisis situations, there are tensions among various ethnic, socio-politico-cultural or religious groups. In most cases, one group or another feels excluded from decision-making processes, causing mistrust and resentment that can fuel further conflict. If diversity in the population is to become an asset rather than a liability, two challenges must be addressed. First, the public service must be inclusive and embrace all groups in the country so that no one feels marginalized. Second, government officials need to tap the potential of every individual to contribute to the performance of the public service. Often this is easier said than done. South Africa, however, successfully managed such a situation and capitalized on its seemingly conflict-prone diversity to create a pluralistic workforce of high-performing public servants.

The public service must be inclusive and embrace all groups in the country so that no one feels marginalized

When the African National Congress came to power in South Africa, it opted to explicitly include all races and both women and men in the country's public service. Restoring legitimacy and credibility by developing a broadly representative public service was seen as key to the transformation process. Early evidence of the ANC's goodwill and reconciliatory tone came with the "sunset provision" in the Interim Constitution of 1993, which protected the tenure of white public servants who had been employed by the apartheid regime. This was followed in 1998 by the White Paper on Affirmative Action, which promoted the employment of previously disadvantaged persons and in particular targeted blacks, women and persons with disabilities. Government departments were also obliged to develop affirmative-action programmes to achieve representivity. All these measures to embrace diversity in the public service helped South Africa become stable relatively quickly.

A representative, merit-based, service-oriented public service can provide a model for participation, inclusive decision-making, reconciliation and social cohesion

A clear message emerges that the composition and functioning of the public service represent a microcosm of a society's overall recovery and mirror the larger governance environment. Thus, a representative, merit-based, service-oriented public service can provide a model for participation, inclusive decision-making, reconciliation and social cohesion, and proactive peacebuilding. Enabling a demographically diverse public service to meet the challenges of recovery and development after conflict requires: (i) sound institutional arrangements for managing the public service; (ii) systems for creating predictability and consistency in the operations of the public service; (iii) laws, rules and regulations that are fair and equitably applied to all public servants; (iv) networks through which public servants can communicate among themselves, with citizens and with external collaborators and partners; and (iv) a commited, competent cadre of public officials with appropriate knowledge, skills (both cognitive and interpersonal), values, norms, attitudes, and behaviour.

Paying civil servants in a post-conflict situation

Most post-conflict countries find themselves with severely strained revenue bases and collection capacities. Therefore, the problems they face in paying their public servants go beyond matters such as how to set different salaries for different job grades. Often, post-conflict countries are not capable of providing any meaningful pay at all. Because such countries need to attract talented people into the public service, the inability to compensate them adequately presents a real challenge.

In addition, most post-conflict countries lack capacities for financial management. While they usually receive financial aid and technical assistance from donors and development partners, this may make it harder for them to manage the payment of public servants in the long term. Donors and development partners often provide and fund large numbers of advisors and consultants who, given the lack of internal capacity, end up doing the work of line managers themselves. In the short-term this offers relief, but it certainly raises concerns about sustainability. Problems also arise when donors and development partners establish projects and recruit local project staff from ministries and government agencies. The donors pay these personnel a fair wage and give them the opportunity to acquire new skills. However, after the projects end, it is difficult for the public service to reabsorb these individuals, because they are more qualified and accustomed to higher pay than the government can offer. Often the income discrepancy between government employees and donor-funded project personnel becomes a source of conflict within the public service.

The situation in the Balkans is illustrative. Experts involved in public administration reform there report the following:

> *Despite the high unemployment in the region, the civil service remains an unattractive option for a professional career because of its politicisation and low salaries. Young people may decide to enter the civil service, if they can count on the right connections, only to leave it shortly afterwards to capitalize, often improperly, on their newly-acquired marketable skills and knowledge. Salary schemes are opaque. Fixed salaries are low, whereas the variable part of the salary tends to be significant. This makes the determination of individual remuneration generally arbitrary, as there are no legitimate performance evaluation schemes in place nor are there the necessary capacities to manage performance-related pay schemes, which have proliferated in the region, often due to advice from international donors ... Well-intentioned policies, by certain donors, to provide salary "top-ups" for key posts related to their interests or their projects have distorted the labour market, created resentment within the public service and have often not resulted in sustainability improvement in capacity. (SIGMA 2004, p. 3).*

To ensure that the actions of donors do not undermine government efforts to manage human resources, both parties should always engage in strategic dialogue. Solutions must be found to the problems

To ensure that the actions of donors do not undermine government efforts to manage human resources, both parties should always engage in strategic dialogue

of low pay for public servants and post-conflict governments' inability to attract the requisite personnel. As part of this problem-solving, donors and development partners should work with the government to design a realistic incentive system that takes into account the country's revenue situation and growth expectations. For example, in Uganda, the incentive scheme was designed to offer public servants progressively better wages as the country's finances improved. Employees would begin by earning a minimum living wage, then be paid an appropriate wage, later earn a wage comparable to others in the region and eventually make a regionally competitive wage. Such an approach helps motivate public servants while ensuring that the government budget does not become overburdened.

Fighting brain drain in post-conflict situations

Once peace and order are re-established, attention can shift to identifying potential returnees and developing appropriate incentives—financial or otherwise—to lure them back

Post-conflict countries lose skilled personnel not only because violence claims many lives but also because fear drives many people to flee their homelands. In 2003 about 30 per cent of all highly educated Sierra Leoneans lived abroad. More than 300 South African specialist nurses are thought to leave the country every month (Tettey 2003). Addressing the problem of brain drain must therefore be part and parcel of any strategy to strengthen human resources in the public service.

To persuade experts to return to post-conflict countries, the first step is to address the factors that forced these experts out originally. Therefore, restoring security and good governance is paramount. Once peace and order are re-established, attention can shift to identifying potential returnees and developing appropriate incentives—financial or otherwise—to lure them back.

Serbia is one country that is currently experimenting with strategies to reverse brain drain. Hoping to ensure steady progress towards European Union accession, Serbia is seeking to convince some of its brightest expatriate scientists, government administrators and academics to return to the country on a temporary or permanent basis. In State institutions alone, there are some 3,700 posts that need to be filled. The Ministry for Diaspora has now created a database of Serbians living abroad who might be interested in returning. Using this database, the International Organization for Migration will work with the University of Belgrade, regional chambers of commerce, and partner institutions in order to attract, place and retain up to 150 returning experts (IOM 2009, p. 87).

While post-conflict countries pursue strategies to draw exiles back home, they should also consider tapping into the pool of émigrés abroad to take advantage of their knowledge and experience. Modern information and communications technology makes it easy to share expertise from afar. Thus skilled members of the diaspora who do not wish to return can still make significant contributions to building human resources capacity in their home countries. The goal is the transformation of diasporic resources into the new "foreign" direct investment. ◆

While post-conflict countries pursue strategies to draw exiles back home, they should also consider tapping into the pool of émigrés abroad to take advantage of their knowledge and experience

4. Lessons learned

- The quality of public servants is crucial to the recovery of a post-conflict government and the trust that people have in it. This makes capacity-building in the public service essential for post-conflict recovery. Strengthening public servants' knowledge, ethics, skills, networks and attitudes is key, because it is through public servants that government services are planned and delivered, critical innovations conceived and realized, needed reforms carried out and trust in government restored.
- The nature of the conflict, the levels of violence and destruction, and the conditions that emerge after the conflict determine the state of human resources in the public service. Reconstruction efforts must be tailored to the specific situation.
- Reconstruction efforts should proceed from an accurate count of a country's public servants and an accurate picture of their knowledge and skills. Because employee censuses are expensive, they should be planned to fit within the overall strategy for developing human resources in the public service. In addition, censuses should be designed for congruence with the local context to ensure that the government has the capacity to effectively use the data collected.
- It is highly desirable for oversight of the recruitment process to be managed by independent bodies such as civil service commissions to avoid cronyism, nepotism, and other forms of favoritism. But because it takes time to create and develop such institutions, interim measures need to be devised to address

the immediate challenge of recruiting competent personnel. If merit-based recruitment is introduced early, there is a greater chance of limiting patronage and other harmful practices and instead ensuring a well-functioning public service.

- Violence takes a toll on civil servants not only in terms of their numbers, but also in terms of their behavior and motivation. To rebuild the ranks of qualified personnel, it is not enough to remedy skills deficits and knowledge gaps. Efforts must also be made to restore integrity, ethics and professional conduct in the public service.

- Diversity within the population should be reflected within the public service. If both men and women, as well as members of all ethnic, religious and other groups, are actively included in the government, then conflict is less likely to erupt. A representative, merit-based, service-oriented public service can provide a model for participation, inclusive decision-making, reconciliation and social cohesion, and proactive peacebuilding.

- Most post-conflict countries lack the financial resources to pay public servants adequately, and reliance on foreign aid and technical assistance is unsustainable in the long term. Donors thus need to work strategically with post-conflict governments to help them develop pay management and incentive systems that will attract the requisite personnel without overtaxing the budget.

Civil war drives many skilled public servants out of their homelands. Addressing the problem of brain drain must therefore be part of the strategy to strengthen human resources in the public service. The first step in convincing professionals to return to post-conflict countries is to restore security and good governance. As a secondary strategy, governments should consider providing financial or other incentives to return to their countries of origin. ◼

Chapter V

Engaging Citizens in Post-conflict Reconstruction:

Decentralization for Participatory Governance

As earlier chapters have noted, post-conflict reconstruction is most successful when all segments of society are engaged in the process. Therefore, as part of their efforts to rebuild robust public administration systems, post-conflict countries must seek to involve citizens in decision-making. One key strategy in this regard is decentralization—the transfer of powers, functions, responsibilities and resources from the central government to local authorities or other subnational entities. In practical terms, decentralization involves striking a balance between the claims of the periphery and the demands of the centre.

This chapter examines decentralization as a mechanism for institutionalizing engaged governance and promoting sustainable peace. It analyzes the concept of decentralization, the challenges in implementing it, and the experiences of several post-conflict countries. The chapter then discusses the importance of engaging two particular constituencies—women and minority groups—in governance, highlighting challenges as well as strategies for success.

1. Decentralization in post-conflict contexts

Overcentralization and monopolization of power by the central government are a source of conflict in many countries. To counteract the tensions caused by elitism and authoritarian rule, many post-conflict governments have implemented decentralization strategies as a means to ensure that services reach communities and that the voices of local people are heard in the development and reconstruction process. When local governance structures exist, citizens and groups can articulate their interests, mediate differences, receive services and exercise legal rights and obligations. Increasingly, decentralization is also regarded as an effective instrument for building and sustaining peace. This is because decentralization creates a situation of engaged governance, where the concern of everyone is not who has power over whom, but how the power is exercised for the well-being of all the people. It is this peaceful power-sharing among all stakeholders that holds the country together.

Decentralization is a key strategy to include citizens in decision-making

However, decentralization does not automatically predispose a country towards peace, democracy or development. If handled poorly and without proper accountability mechanisms, decentralization can reallocate power and resources in a way that leads to power struggles, thereby creating instability or even renewed conflict.

All the same, there is a case for designing decentralized systems in post-conflict countries. Decentralization provides a structural arrangement for the orderly negotiation and shared exercise of power, and it facilitates the involvement of the local people in policy decisions about their country's development. Moreover, it offers a means of allocating resources effectively, improving service delivery and enhancing the prospects for peace.

If handled poorly decentralization can create instability. Correctly, it promotes improved service delivery and better peace prospects

Horizontal decentralization

Decentralization can take two forms. Under *vertical decentralization*, the central government hands down certain powers, functions and resources to local governments. Under *horizontal decentralization*, governance responsibilities are spread more broadly across the society, and civil society organizations (non-governmental organizations, religious organizations, community groups, etc.) are empowered to plan and manage affairs themselves. There is a concerted effort to involve all citizens in public administraton, including women, people with disabili-

Vertical decentralization promotes participation by representation

ties, youth and other groups that were marginalized before the eruption of conflict. With horizontal decentralization, multiple constituents participate in formulating policies, identifying priorities, planning actions, budgeting and implementating and monitoring programs.

It is important to clarify that vertical decentralization also offers opportunities for citizens to participate in government decision-making—but indirectly, through their elected representatives. In order to promote direct community engagement, vertical decentralization needs to be accompanied by horizontal decentralization. The latter enables people to exert regular influence on their leaders to shape their decisions and demand accountability from them. Indeed, horizontal decentralization requires "structuring local governments in such a way that they are legally obliged to seek and promote the participation of local communities" in making and implementing decisions (Kauzya 2007a, p. 5). The underlying concept is that community members have more experience and knowledge about their needs than anyone else, and therefore they are in the best position to devise appropriate responses.

Horizontal decentralization is when vote is reinforced by voice and direct participation

Elements of successful decentralization

Decentralization is an ongoing process requiring legal frameworks, strengthened capacity, accountability, and engagement

Decentralization is not a one-time action but an ongoing process that requires innovative ways of structuring and institutionalizing the interface between people and their local governments. The elements of successful participatory governance at the local level include the following:

- Legal frameworks and structural arrangements to devolve power not only to local governments but also to local communities;
- Strengthened local government capacity to perform governance functions (including revenue generation, provision of local services, personnel management, planning and decision-making, government performance monitoring, investment management for development, and local fiscal management);
- Local government responsiveness and accountability to both citizens and the central government (evidenced by transparency, dissemination of information to the public, accessibility of public meetings and records, etc.);
- Enhanced role for civil society, with civil society organizations and the private sector working in partnership with local and national governments; and
- Evidence of government intent to improve the quality of life in local communities, and demonstrable progress in doing so. ◆

2. Challenges in decentralizing

After conflict, it is through local governments that citizens receive basic services and goods. But effective service delivery is not the only responsibility that local governments have to the communities they serve. They also need to provide a means for citizens to participate in the post-conflict reconstruction of the economic, political and social fabric of the country. Decentralization may present ideal opportunities to create a new basis for state-society relations.

However, this is a mammoth task, because local structures "are often at the frontlines of fighting between warring sides and may be destroyed during conflict" (United Nations Peacebuilding Commission 2007b, p. 2).

Because of the diversity of post-conflict scenarios, it is impossible to make an exhaustive list of the challenges involved in decentralizing. However, under no circumstances can decentralization be initiated without political will. This means that central government leaders must be committed to sharing power and authority. In addition, civil servants must be ready and willing to facilitate the transfer of power, authority, functions, responsibilities and resources. Lack of bureaucratic buy-in can derail decentralization policies. Yet central government officials often do resist the decentralization process, suspecting that it will mean some loss of power for them. To overcome this attitudinal constraint, it is important to conceive decentralization policies with the extensive involvement of civil servants at the national level. They need to understand the policy objectives, implementation plans and coordination roles, as well as the benefits of the reforms.

Central government leaders must be committed to sharing power and authority

Another challenge in decentralizing is ensuring that civil society has sufficient capacity and will to responsibly handle the power transferred to it from the central government. Experience shows that local communities, particularly those traumatized by conflict, do not always accept decentralization policies automatically. In countries used to highly centralized governance, people are accustomed to receiving services from the central government, and so they tend to perceive decentralization as a move by the State to abandon its service provision role and neglect the people. Governments must therefore clarify the objectives and benefits of decentralization and undertake local capacity development.

It is also imperative to implement decentralization carefully so that local elites cannot abuse their authority over local resources. Otherwise, local corruption can pose a serious threat to post-conflict reconstruction. Another challenge in decentralizing is the expense. The costs associated with creating additional layers of governance can be significant for post-conflict countries with few resources. Security concerns and mistrust between the central power and local actors may also limit the effectiveness and extent of citizen participation in local government structures, hampering social reconciliation and development efforts.

Finally, it is worth mentioning some challenges identified by an expert panel organized by the United Nations Peacebuilding Commission (2007a, p. 2). These include:

- Inappropriate or ambiguous legal frameworks that fail to provide guidance on the relationship of local authority to the central government, the services it should deliver, and how it can raise and distribute revenue;
- Weak institutional frameworks for implementing the existing legal frameworks;
- Political and social dynamics that, if not taken into account, can result in failure, since successful decentralization in post-conflict societies depends on repairing social cohesion as well as rebuilding institutions; and
- Difficulty identifying legitimate local authorities to deal with, since it may not be clear who holds power or who is a trustworthy partner. ◆

3. Decentralization experiences in selected countries

Strategies need to be tailored to specific circumstances

Decentralization strategies need to be tailored to the specific circumstances of every country, especially in the case of states recovering from devastating conflict. Although approaches will vary according to the local context, it is instructive to study what has—and hasn't— worked in the past. Therefore, we briefly examine the experiences of six conflict-torn countries—four in Africa (South Africa, Rwanda,

Uganda and Mozambique) and two in Latin America (El Salvador and Guatemala)—that have used decentralization to promote participatory governance.

South Africa

In 1994 South Africa's first democratically elected government initiated a post-conflict recovery process. In response to popular demand for decentralization, the Government undertook an extensive negotiation process that went on alongside negotiations for a post-apartheid national constitution. The negotiations were crucial for mobilizing all South Africans to accept the principle of empowering local communities and dismantling the apartheid system that had left the country with racially divided business and residential areas. The new legal framework required each municipality to prepare an Integrated Development Plan created with the participation of the entire municipality and all stakeholders.

South Africa established legal frameworks requiring people's participation in municipal development planning

The structural arrangement that facilitated the formulation of these plans was the Integrated Development Plan Representative Forum. Forum participants included local council members, traditional community leaders, senior officials from municipal government departments, representatives from organized stakeholder groups and various resource people. The Forum provided a structure for discussion, negotiation and joint decision-making. It also ensured proper communication between all stakeholders and the municipality, as well as monitoring of planning and implementation processes. Community members felt empowered to participate and influence the social, political and economic decisions that concern them. Thus the Forum structure institutionalized participatory decision-making in local governments and enhanced peaceful interaction.

Rwanda

In Rwanda, unlike South Africa, the push to decentralize came from the top. After the genocidal conflict in 1994, the Government undertook decentralization as part of peacebuilding. Old politico-administrative structures, leadership groups and mentalities were replaced by new ones more suited to promoting peace and social reconciliation. Participatory decision-making, based on local leadership, was encouraged through the establishment of Community Development Committees (CDCs) attended by all community members of voting age.

Rwanda encouraged participatory decision-making based on local leadership

Gender issues were also mainstreamed in development planning, and it was initially mandated that women should represent 33 per cent of local government council representatives.

Although political will was responsible for initiating the decentralization, civic will was cultivated through extensive consultation and sensitization. Community development was conceived as a dynamic process in which members of a given community analyze their environment, define their needs and problems, elaborate collective and individual plans to address them, and implement the plans using community resources complemented, where necessary, by resources provided by the central government or private sector organizations (Kauzya 2007a). CDCs were instrumental in engaging the community with its own development and efforts to reduce poverty. Community members submitted proposals to the local government council and shared responsibility for monitoring, evaluating and controlling development activities. Emphasis was given to accountability, transparency, responsiveness of the public administration, sustainable capacity development at the local level, and efficient service delivery.

Uganda

Uganda established participatory decision making at community level, quotas for women and marginalized groups' representation

After 1986, Uganda enacted substantial decentralization reforms that were engineered from the top through consultations and pilot programmes. The reforms were aimed at enhancing State capacity and avoiding continued conflict arising from ethnic divisions. A pilot decentralization exercise in 13 districts, conducted in 1993, helped obtain support for broader decentralization. Participatory governance at the local level was also recognized by the 1995 constitution.

As in Rwanda, participatory decision-making was instituted at the community level. Uganda's Local Government Statute provided the legal basis for establishing village-based councils composed of all villagers of voting age, led by an elected chairperson and an executive. Quotas mandated that women must represent one-third of the representatives in local councils, and other formerly marginalized groups must be represented as well.

Decentralization was beneficial for peacebuilding, as it strengthened institutions, increased citizen participation in development, encouraged accountability through improved local monitoring, and improved service delivery. Policy shifts in the implementation of decentralization have also started addressing local economic development in order to create more employment opportunities, increase local incomes and expand the local revenue base (Mutabwire 2008). However, some challenges remain. Uganda needs to reduce administrative fragmentation and expand decentralization to the whole country (Northern Uganda only recently brokered peace). Moreover, there is a need to accommodate political competition while encouraging a shift away from ethnically based political identifications, which have been so contentious in the past (HPCR n.d.).

Mozambique

The 1992 Rome Peace Accord marked the end of a 16-year civil war that affected almost all of Mozambique, destroying the social fabric of the country and marginalizing much of the population. Soon after, in 1994, consensus started to emerge on the need for a political framework characterized by inclusion and geared towards poverty reduction to ensure long-lasting peace. Political inclusion was understood to require political and administrative decentralization in the country. Accordingly, a legal framework for establishing local governance was developed in the constitution and in Law 2/97.

In Mozambique, the lack of strong political will in support of inclusionary strategies has slowed down decentralization

However, because of disagreements between the leading and opposition parties, only a fraction of the country's municipalities were allowed to elect their own leaders and form local governments. In most of the country, subnational power remains concentrated at the district level, where officials are appointed by the central government and not legitimated by the local communities. Furthermore, local governments lack mechanisms to raise their own resources. Sitoe and Hunguana (2005, p. 13) conclude that decentralization in Mozambique "is not yet a clear expression of political will geared towards the consolidation of democratic governance in the country". However, decentralization has allowed some citizens to become active participants in governing their cities or townships—most notably in the municipality of Dondo.

El Salvador

The Government of El Salvador, supported by the national association of municipalities, promoted decentralization and community participation immediately after signing the Peace Accords in 1992. The aim, after 12 years of civil war, was to embark on a peacebuilding and unification process whereby the Government would regain citizens' trust, be more responsive to their needs and encourage citizen participation in government decision-making by gradually moving towards decentralization. This entailed the creation of more autonomous and inclusive municipal governments.

El Salvasdor recognized the need for promoting citizen participation mechanisms

Since 1992, when the key policy directions were established, some progress has been made (Pereira 2003). With international support, programmes were piloted to foster community participation in identifying priorities, developing local plans, and defining local service requirements; these programmes engaged citizens through mechanisms such as budget hearings and radio talk shows. Participatory strategic planning processes were also replicated nationwide and made a condition for financing infrastructure projects.

Challenges included changing individual, group and institutional attitudes to be more favorable towards participatory governance. For instance, most mayors were willing to hold the public hearings mandated for municipalities to become eligible for central government funds, but they were not initially inclined to involve the community in key policy decisions. Similarly, municipal councils were originally slow to accept the idea of citizen advisory groups.

Guatemala

In Guatemala, rules for participation have been created, but their implementation has lagged behind

Peace accords were signed in Guatemala in 1999 at the end of 36 years of conflict and authoritarian rule. The Guatemalan case is informative because of the "extraordinary degree to which decentralization is associated with the incorporation of civil society generally, and long-marginalized indigenous populations in particular, into the decision making processes of government" (Bland 2002, p. 1).

As part of the peace agreement, the Government agreed to reform the municipal code to ensure local input into local decisions through the *cabildo abierto*—the Guatemalan equivalent of the town meeting. The Government also committed to restoring local development councils, in view of their important role in ensuring that community groups—associations of indigenous people, campesino organizations, women's groups, etc.—participate in the formulation of local investment priorities. Municipal technical and planning units were also considered to be instrumental for establishing a dialogue with local organizations and communities and promoting participatory means of addressing municipal concerns, prioritizing projects and reaching consensus on investments.

Guatemala thus created multiple opportunities for citizens and civil society groups to interact with the State. The emphasis on citizen participation has helped prevent or resolve some conflicts and laid the foundations for a more peaceful society. However, "the legal reforms that have formally opened space for citizen participation in municipal affairs have not had, in practice, the desired impact" (Bland 2002, p. 3). The local development councils have been criticized as complex and difficult to implement. Mayors are reluctant to convene town meetings, and in any case, they are not obligated to act on community input they receive. Municipalities lack autonomy because the functions of different levels of government are not clearly defined. Thus the Guatemalan Government needs to go beyond the creation of participatory mechanisms and move towards institutionalizing them. ◆

4. Engaging women in governance: Challenges and strategies

Typically during conflict, as men are drawn into the fighting, women take on new roles as community leaders or non-traditional workers. However, once the conflict ends, stereotypical attitudes about women's capacities for leadership and decision-making often resurface. Research shows that "during and immediately after the conflict there is an expansion of women's roles in the public arena that is often followed by a decrease in women's opportunities and a retraction of women's space for public action in the post conflict stages of reconstruction" (Mutamba and Izabiliza 2005, p. 9). *www.peacebuildinginitiative.org.*

Women should not be viewed as mere victims of conflict: they are leaders in rebuilding communities

Traditionally, women were viewed as mere victims of conflict. The fact that they were effective local leaders—actively engaged in rebuilding communities, mediating, promoting peace, rehabilitating victims and overcoming trauma—remained largely undocumented. As a result, despite their vital contributions during the conflict and recovery periods, women were excluded from the negotiating tables and left out of the ensuing peacebuilding processes. In Mozambique, to cite just one example, women played a critical role during the liberation struggle that brought independence to the country, but they were totally absent from the Rome peace process that ended the civil war.

Peace cannot be lasting unless both men and women can participate in peacebuilding

Arguably, peace cannot be lasting unless both men and women can participate in peacebuilding, influence reconstruction and development efforts and equally enjoy their benefits. Gender-specific issues need to be addressed as part of the formal post-conflict decision-making process in order to affect policy and programming development. This principle is reflected in Security Council resolution 1889 (S/RES/1889 – 5 October 2009) which urges Member States, United Nations bodies, donors and civil society to ensure that "women's empowerment is taken into account during post-conflict needs assessments and planning, and factored into subsequent funding disbursements and programme activities (..)". Hence, both men and women need to be participants, voicing their respective needs and priorities on an equal basis within a spirit of coexistence, nonviolence and inclusiveness.

Unfortunately, the exclusion of women from decision-making processes means that their needs and concerns may be neglected. "As a result, resources may be inaccurately targeted and the protection problems women and girls face regarding their security and their access to services may be exacerbated" (UNHCR 2008). The absence of gender perspectives may significantly slow down reconstruction activities, jeopardize democratic inclusiveness and lasting peace, and further erode women's power within fragile and divided societies. This ultimately has negative effects on economic growth, prosperity, the recovery of human capital and overall development.

The Beijing Platform of Action states that women need to be part of decision-making and leadership

Therefore, special attention must be paid to engaging women in post-conflict reconstruction. This is a position that the United Nations advocated at the Fourth World Conference on Women, held in Beijing in September 1995. The Beijing Platform for Action stated that women should be assured of equal access to and full participation in power structures and decision-making, and that efforts should be made to increase women's capacity to participate in decision-making and leadership. The Platform also highlighted the importance of gender balance in governmental bodies and in public administration. These provisions were reaffirmed in 2000 by United Nations Security Council resolution 1325, and by world leaders at the 2005 World Summit.

Challenges impeding women's participation

Many post-conflict contexts are characterized by unequal power-sharing between men and women. Women often have the burden of ensuring the subsistence of their households—they are frequently the sole breadwinners, struggling to provide food and water under difficult security conditions. They are also the primary caregivers for elderly relatives and children, and often, as in Rwanda, for displaced people and orphans. This is a responsibility made more arduous by the injuries and disease commonly suffered during conflict. Because of the heavy demands on them, the majority of women have very limited opportunities to get involved in national or even local decision-making.

In addition to increased care burdens, women also experience lack of empowerment and equal rights. They are often denied access to land and other property, for example, which has a detrimental effect on power relations between men and women.

According to the Peacebuilding Initiative, even when "women's rights and priorities have been incorporated in peace agreements and post-conflict legislative and policy reform, these formal measures do not necessarily translate into better access for women to decision-making processes, nor to increased protection from violence at the community level". URL: *www.peacebuildinginitiative.org*. As acknowledged in United Nations Security Council resolution 1820, persistent violence, intimidation and discrimination are additional obstacles to women's participation and full involvement in post-conflict public life.

It must be noted that women are not a monolithic group and their needs are not homogeneous. In post-conflict societies in particular, women may be divided by competition for resources and by tensions over tribal affiliation, ethnic identity, religious affiliation or social status. Such divisions diminish trust among women, which weakens collective efforts to incorporate their needs and rights within new social structural, economic, political and social frameworks.

Women may be divided by competition. This weakens collective efforts to incorporate their needs and rights

Lastly, women's participation in public administration is hampered by a lack of opportunities for women to network and develop formal leadership skills. In Rwanda, for example, women were traditionally not encouraged to attend political gatherings or speak in public. The society was highly patriarchal, and women were accustomed to expressing themselves indirectly through another person, preferably a man. In addition, they often lacked the education or information to feel confident publicly voicing their ideas (Mutamba and Izabiliza 2005).

Women lack opportunities to network and develop leadership skills

Box V.1 **Rwanda's success in engaging women in governance**

Rwanda's 1994 war and genocide, which caused loss of life and destruction of the country's socio-economic and political infrastructure, had a disproportionately strong impact on women. Thousands of women suffered rape, physical injury, and other traumas, including infection with the AIDS virus. Widows had to become heads of households and caretakers of orphans, despite severe economic deprivation. Nonetheless, women became a driving force of peacebuilding, reconciliation and socio-economic development, thanks to committed leadership at different levels and the willingness of the people to move forward.

From the very beginning of the post-conflict period, the Government of Rwanda gave priority to promoting gender equality and women's empowerment as a prerequisite for sustainable peace and development. It established a national mechanism to ensure women's engagement in the reconstruction process, and as part of this mechanism, it created the Ministry of Family and Women's Affairs. Among the priorities of the Ministry was the establishment of women's committees that ran from the lowest administrative level (cell) up to the national level. The overall objective of these committees was to allow Rwandese women to express their views, concerns and interests regarding the country's reconstruction processes. The Government further demonstrated its trust in women by appointing them to positions of leadership in the executive, legislative and judiciary branches.

Because of this enabling environment, women started actively participating in decision-making and managing financial resources, despite their inexperience in these non-traditional roles. Women in leadership positions created associations to influence reforms in politics, law, elections, justice and security. For instance, the Rwanda Women Leaders' Caucus lobbied for laws protecting women's rights (relating to inheritances, children, the workplace, etc.). A caucus of female parliamentarians mobilized grassroots women to help shape the constitution of 2003, which gave special focus to the principles of national unity and gender equality. Women were granted at least 30 per cent of posts in decision-making organs. The Government also set up national women's councils to give women more visibility and influence in the national debate on reconstruction policy. In addition, decentralization facilitated the representation of women at the district, provincial and community levels.

At the same time, networks of women's groups were instrumental in creating opportunities for reconciliation. Some of these opportunities came from income-generating activities, particularly in rural areas, that not only empowered women economically but helped restore trust and harmony within the community. As women worked together, they broke barriers of isolation and mistrust, particularly between families who survived the genocide and those whose relatives were suspected of committing genocide.

Women also played an important role in the peacebuilding process. They helped bring an early end to the insurgency by switching their support from the rebels to the Government and persuading their sons and husbands to return home peacefully. Women also engaged in negotiations and "peace talks" with other associations inside and outside Rwanda, reaching consensus to focus on peace.

Source: Mutamba and Izabiliza (2005)

Strategies for engaging women

Strategies include decentralization, and setting quotas for participation in decision-making

A number of countries have made a concerted effort to empower women and widen opportunities for their participation in the post-conflict reconstruction process. For example, governments have instituted decentralization policies, as discussed earlier in the chapter, to make governance opportunities available at the local level. They have passed laws, adopted constitutional provisions and enacted electoral, judicial and military reforms aimed at ending gender discrimination and opening more doors for women.

Another effective strategy to bring women into public administration is to set quotas for their participation. Rwanda, for example, mandated that 30 per cent of the positions in government decision-making bodies be filled by female representatives. (For a review of Rwanda's comprehensive efforts to engage women in governance, see box V.1.) Uganda's 1995 Constitution states that women should make up one-third of the membership of each local government council. The introduction of quotas in Burundi resulted in women comprising 30 per cent of parliamentarians and seven of 20 ministers in 2006. For the first time, women were also elected as chiefs of communes (Klot 2007).

As women were a driving force in peacebuilding, some countries prioritized gender equality by establishing gender mechanisms

Quotas—whether voluntarily adopted by political parties or constitutionally or legislatively mandated—have certainly helped women gain access to leadership positions. However, greater female representation does not necessarily equate to higher empowerment. Gender quotas tend to reduce concerns about women's participation to a superficial, numerical approach. It is important to know whether a country is truly committed to involving women in governance or just filling its mandatory quotas. In Sudan, Congo and Uganda, for example, women activists criticized affirmative-action programmes they felt were implemented simply to draw donor funding and media coverage. The programmes, they argued, were vague, inappropriate, poorly monitored and not sustainable (see the Peacebuilding Initiative[15]). According to a UNIFEM[16] study on women, war and peace, "quotas must be seen as a temporary solution to increase gender balance ... They are a first step on the path to gender equality, both a practical and a symbolic measure to support women's leadership".

Beyond the use of quotas, a crucial step is to enhance women's leadership capacity. In this regard, greater partnership with existing women's organizations can be an important strategy. Civil society women's groups provide avenues for advocacy, mobilization and social networking. They thus widen opportunities to advance gender mainstreaming, on the one hand, and offer opportunities for women to practise leadership, on the other. In addition, capacity-building can be done by government agencies that focus on improving women's lives. Some countries, for example, establish a Ministry of Women's Affairs, Ministry of Gender Equality or a State Secretary for Women. In certain circumstances, temporary units that oversee the immediate post-conflict needs of women can also contribute to developing women's leadership capacity.

ICT can foster women's participation

Finally, the application of information and communication technologies in public administration and governance can help women participate in decision-making. This is a particularly useful strategy when

Quotas have limits. They must be seen as temporary solutions to increase gender balance

---

[15] Beyond victimhood", 2006, 16
[16] Syrleaf and Rehn, "Women War peace", 2002, 81

security concerns restrict physical mobility, as happens often in post-conflict situations. In such circumstances, "cyber centers" can provide women with access to Internet resources in a safe environment. ◆

5. Engaging minority groups in governance: Challenges and strategies

Exclusion of minority groups can hamper reconstruction and development processes

Just as it is vital for women to participate in post-conflict governance, so it is vital to engage minority groups, particularly in multi-ethnic, multi-cultural societies. The State "must be a polity that is shared by all citizens of the country" (Daskalovski 2007, p. 207). When a group of citizens does not identify with the symbols, legal systems and institutions of a State, its legitimacy is critically undermined. This triggers social unrest that can slow down reconstruction and development processes or even escalate into violent conflict.

Minority groups, by virtue of being in the minority, are always at high risk of becoming marginalized by the dominant groups in society. If their perspectives and needs are not taken into consideration during post-conflict reconstruction, then policies and programmes designed to address the needs of the majority can prevent them from enjoying peace dividends and can even harm their interests. In the mid- to long term, marginalizing certain groups can cause imbalances in economic and social development that lead to structural socio-economic disparities and mounting unrest, especially when coupled with uneven resource allocation within a country.

Challenges impeding the participation of minority groups

Exclusion can derive from lack of respect for cultural identity or unequal access to resources

When a country has a diverse population, differences in ethnicity, religion and culture can create tensions. Some groups may feel socially excluded and aggrieved by a perceived lack of respect for their cultural identity and heritage. In other cases, conflicts arise over control of resources or access to opportunities. In Indonesia, for example, various ethnic groups clashed over ownership rights to local land and forests. They felt threatened by a lack of transparent government practices in allocating mining and forestry rights and by the arbitrary setting of territorial boundaries (Hadi 2005).

The potential for mistrust between communities intensifies as they become more ethnically or religiously homogenous, especially if there are few channels for communication between different groups. Creating separate political districts as a way of dealing with issues of power-sharing and resource allocation only increases the risk of conflict, as stronger religious and ethnic lines are drawn.

Decentralization can increase conflict when religious and ethnic lines are drawn by dividing power along these lines

When violent conflict has an ethnic or religious dimension, social cohesion can be profoundly damaged, but the bonds within ethnic or religious groups can actually be strengthened, thus the social pressures that led to or emerged during the conflict continue to affect socio-politico-economic life even after the formal cessation of hostilities. Several post-conflict transitional governments have sought to achieve social cohesion by dividing power among different ethnic or religious groups. However, "constituting a government along these lines, especially in societies where such identities have previously not been sharply drawn, or where different groups have suffered from relatively unequal access to opportunity, may heighten division among groups" (United Nations 2007, p. 15).

The question, then, is what should States do to reconcile and bring together antagonistic communities polarized along religious or ethnic lines? How can governments engage them in rebuilding and developing the country for the good of all?

Strategies for engaging minority groups

Studies conducted by the United Nations show that local governance can give voice to the local population and enhance their participation in reconstruction and peacebuilding efforts, Thus decentralization, as discussed earlier in the chapter, is a key strategy for helping minority groups become invested in post-conflict public administration. And if power and responsibilities are to be shared, then decentralization must be accompanied by capacity development for members of marginalized groups. Training and education should focus on leadership development, partnership building and conflict management and resolution.

Sharing a common purpose can help put the public good above group interests

When local governance is firmly established, political leaders need to create platforms aimed at engaging citizens in community dialogue and participatory decision-making to ensure social cohesion and ethnic harmony. Religious, traditional and community leaders are among the non-state actors who can help foster dialogue and reconciliation. Working to-

Minority groups' participation must be promoted through laws and regulations

gether, civil society actors and public officials can create what Chapter III called "an infrastructure for peace"—mechanisms, systems and processes that stimulate dialogue and help solve day-to-day disputes within society. The trust and participation of minority groups cannot be taken for granted, however; it needs to be nurtured. To bring about social cohesion, efforts must be made to strengthen a sense of national identity forged around shared goals and values rather than affiliation with a particular ethnic group, tribe or religious group. Local governments can also promote social integration by organizing cultural festivals, sports contests and traditional folklore and music performances, as well as collectively supported initiatives. When people feel themselves to be part of a joint enterprise working towards a common purpose, they are more willing to put the public good above the interests of their own group.

A key to creating social cohesion is rebuilding inter-community and inter-ethnic dialogue and trust

A key to creating such social cohesion is rebuilding inter-community and inter-ethnic dialogue and trust. One promising strategy involves community-led reconciliation and recovery programmes that help communities mend relations and move towards peace by rediscovering their "interconnected nature and responsibility for each other's welfare" (Pottebaum and Lee 2007, p. 4).

Post-conflict leaders must also "proactively address the root causes of conflict and diminish tension and destructive competition among interest groups" (United Nations 2007, p. 16). This is not a task for the government alone; civil society groups can make major contributions to identifying, analyzing and addressing the causes of conflict. Their engagement is critical to ensure that actions are responsive to people's needs, and that all segments of the population take ownership of the solutions and share responsibility for sustaining them.

In many cases, enactment or revision of laws and regulations is needed to promote minority groups' participation in public administration. For example, after the violent conflict in 2001 between different ethnic groups in the Former Yugoslav Republic of Macedonia (FYROM), the Government took legal steps to ensure the minority rights of ethnic Albanians. Among other things, the principle of ethnic neutrality was incorporated into the constitution. New rules in Parliament required that "laws affecting an ethnic minority population must be passed by the majority of members of that ethnicity, in addition to an overall majority" (Daskalovski 2007, p. 206). In addition, special measures were implemented to achieve greater representation of minority groups in public office at both the national and local levels.

Governments may also create special structures to engage minority groups in governance. Guatemala, for example, set up a system of urban and rural development councils as the main means for the Maya, Xinca, Garifuna and non-indigenous population to participate in public administration.

Indonesia used a combination of strategies to encourage minority group participation after the collapse of President Suharto's regime in 1998. Minorities had been marginalized for decades, and ethnic or religious conflict affected several parts of Indonesia, particularly the eastern provinces. The Government of Indonesia National Mid-Term Development Plan (2004-2009) identified stronger social trust and harmony among community groups as a priority. One of the focus areas of the Plan was increased community participation in public policymaking and overcoming social problems (Hadi 2005). The new legal framework gave full autonomy to (rural) districts and (urban) municipalities to manage a number of services and duties, and it clarified the fiscal roles and responsibilities of central, provincial and local governments. Key responsibilities for local development and community welfare were assigned to local governments, with the goal of attaining social cohesion and ending sectarian tensions through strengthened vertical and horizontal relationships. This prompted the institution of a village council, called a *Badan Perwakilan Desa*, which was responsible for drafting village regulation and overseeing the budget. This structure proved instrumental in achieving decentralization objectives in those instances where its members represented different village groups.

Research conducted in the country identified the municipality of Solo—located in Central Java province, 60 kilometers from the city of Yogyakarta—as an example of best practice (Widianingsih 2006). This municipality needed to address a high level of diversity that contributed to conflict and social disintegration. To do so, the local government, in collaboration with non-governmental organizations and civil society organizations, adopted in 2001 a model of direct community involvement in development planning. This approach eased tensions in the city by emphasizing citizens' rights to equality and freedom of expression through participatory development. This helped foster better relations among different ethnic groups, and despite practical problems, community involvement continued to increase in 2003 and 2004. ◆

Special governance structures, participation in policy making and development planning are key to effective decentralized governance

6. Lessons learned

- Participatory governance at the local level facilitates the involvement of local communities in policy decisions about their own development, thereby creating a shared commitment to peaceful progress that reduces the likelihood of violent conflict.
- Successful decentralization depends on political will, civic will and capacity development at the local level and careful implementation to ensure appropriate power-sharing arrangements and allocation of resources.
- Peace cannot be lasting unless both men and women participate in shaping post-conflict reconstruction and are able to equally enjoy its benefits. Barriers to women's participation include traditional notions about gender roles, women's caregiving burdens and their inexperience in leadership positions. Nonetheless, women's participation can be increased by enacting reforms to end gender discrimination, setting quotas for female representation in government and undertaking capacity development efforts to strengthen women's leadership skills.
- Peace cannot be lasting unless minority groups are engaged in post-conflict governance, especially when ethnic or religious divisions were a root cause of the conflict or a contributing factor. It is important to foster dialogue and reconciliation among antagonistic groups, build a shared national identity that trumps ethnic or religious ties, and take concrete steps (such as constitutional reforms or the creation of special mechanisms) to protect minority rights and engage minority groups in participatory decision-making. ■

Chapter VI

Promoting Citizen-Centric Public Service Delivery in Post-Conflict Situations

This chapter looks at the challenges and strategies involved in rebuilding capacities for public service delivery. In particular, the chapter analyses the benefits of a multi-stakeholder approach and the crucial role that information and communication technologies (ICTs) can play.

The fundamental raison d'être of government is the delivery of services to its people. These include social services (primary education and basic health services), infrastructure (water and sanitation, roads and bridges) and services that promote personal security (justice system and police services), whether provided directly by the public sector or by government-financed private providers.

Unfortunately, during times of violent conflict, attention and resources shift from production to destruction. The processes and mechanisms by which a society produces public, private and social goods and services are severely impaired, and because the government can no longer deliver public services reliably, its credibility and legitimacy are eroded. Consequently, restoring the delivery of public services after violent conflict is not just a matter of ensuring the population's survival, but also a vehicle for re-establishing public trust in government. Furthermore, improving service provision will reduce tensions and grievances among groups struggling to meet basic needs. In this way, effective delivery of public services contributes to peace and stability, which in turn facilitates economic development, as shown in figure VI.1.

Restoring the delivery of public services after violent conflict is not just a matter of ensuring the population's survival, but also a vehicle for re-establishing public trust in government

Political, social and religious leaders all need to be strongly committed to the interests of their country in order to develop a shared national vision and manage people's expectations. Governments should explain that the vision cannot be realized immediately, but that the country is moving forward. To the extent possible, leaders should pursue redistributive policies, as failure to do so increases the risk of violent resolution of disputes. Furthermore, although national leaders are unquestionably responsible for establishing reconstruction priorities and implementing strategies, they should seek solid partnerships.

Figure VI.1 **Virtuous cycle of state legitimacy, effectiveness and public service delivery**

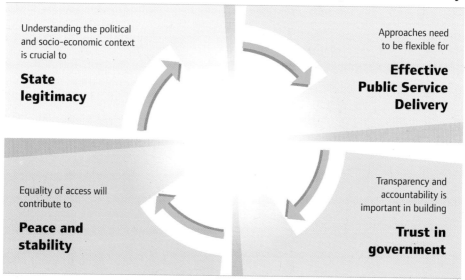

Understanding the political and socio-economic context is crucial to

State legitimacy

Approaches need to be flexible for

Effective Public Service Delivery

Equality of access will contribute to

Peace and stability

Transparency and accountability is important in building

Trust in government

Table VI.1 **Erosion of public services and effects on the population in conflict-torn countries**

Country	Service erosion and its effects
Bosnia and Herzegovina	During the fighting in 1994, fewer than 35 per cent of children were immunized, compared with 95 per cent before hostilities broke out. After the war, 50 per cent of schools required repair or reconstruction.
Kosovo	After the war, 65 per cent of schools required repair or reconstruction., Bosnia and Herzegovina and, respectively, 65, 50 and 45 percent of schools required repair or reconstruction after war.
Liberia	During the 15-year civil war, at least 50 per cent of all schools were destroyed, depriving 800,000 children of education.
Mozambique	After the war, 45 per cent of schools required repair or reconstruction
Nicaragua	In 1985–1986, a measles epidemic was attributed in large part to the declining ability of the health service to immunize those at risk in conflict-affected areas.
Rwanda	As people fled the violence in 1994, 6–10 per cent of those arriving in Zaire (now the Democratic Republic of the Congo) died within a month from cholera, dysentery and other diseases caused by lack of access to safe water. The crude death rate of 20–35 per 10,000 population per day was two or three times higher than that previously reported in refugee populations.
Timor-Leste	An estimated 95 per cent of classrooms were destroyed or severely damaged in the violent aftermath of the 1999 referendum on independence.

Sources: WHO (2002), p. 223; Ibrahim Index of African Governance.
http://www.moibrahimfoundation.org/The%20full%202008%20Ibrahim%20Index.pdf.
Accessed 12 August 2009.

In post-conflict situations, ICT networks can be extremely useful in accurately mapping the areas where humanitarian relief, security services, health care, education, water services, etc., should be targeted

A State's ability to deliver public services will depend on a number of factors, including the current social, economic and political conditions, the level of security within the country, and the adequacy of available resources, including the personnel, skills, systems and infrastructure to deliver services. Because violent conflict usually results in a loss of assets and a corresponding reduction in economic production, post-conflict governments and their development partners face particular challenges in delivering public services. They have meager financial, human and material resources, as well as dilapidated infrastructure and facilities. Moreover, because violence can destroy a country's educational infrastructure and prevent children from acquiring the knowledge and skills they need to become productive workers, conflict can seriously impede long-term economic recovery and development. Table VI.1 highlights some of the effects of conflict on social services and infrastructure in selected countries. ◆

1. The challenges of delivering citizen-centric services after conflict

Post-conflict countries face an array of challenges related to the delivery of services. These are challenges not only for the authorities in the affected countries but also for the donors and development partners trying to support them.

The particular needs and issues will vary by country, of course. In some cases, the public sector has collapsed as a result of the conflict. In other cases, the public sector is functioning but struggling to cope with regime change, lingering violence, disputes over resources, lack of funds, etc. Typically, however, regardless of context, the following questions arise:

- How can public services be delivered with severely impaired institutional, human, material, infrastructural and financial capacities? (See box VI.1 for a description of the obstacles that Sierra Leone faced, for example.)
- How can public services be delivered effectively and efficiently in a situation where accountability systems are not yet robust and people are more concerned with individual survival than with delivering services to all citizens?
- How can providers of public services meet the high public expectations that always accompany new regimes after conflict?
- How can efforts and resources for public service delivery be spread to all corners of the country and all population groups, to avoid the perception that the government is delivering public services to select segments of the population?
- How can the short-term need to provide services, especially to the poor (who in most post-conflict countries are the majority), be balanced with the long-term needs for public sector reform, economic recovery and development, all of which compete for attention and resources? If the focus is on meeting short-term needs, there may be inadequate resources for future generations, thus sowing the seeds of future conflict.

A special challenge in the delivery of public services is that of infrastructure deficiencies. In post-conflict situations, ICT networks can be extremely useful in accurately mapping the areas where

Box VI.1 **Post-conflict rebuilding in Sierra Leone**

The social and economic impact of the 10-year civil conflict in Sierra Leone was devastating. An estimated 20,000 people were killed and thousands more injured or maimed. Over 2 million people were displaced (500,000 fled to neighboring countries). Skilled professionals flocked to Freetown or fled the country, leaving most of Sierra Leone drained of skilled workers. Most of the country's social, economic and physical infrastructure was destroyed. Local community social and productive infrastructure such as markets, stores, rice mills, and community service buildings were completely vandalized.

The conflict also devastated the already-limited social services. An estimated 50 per cent of health and educational facilities were destroyed. Death or migration of trained health staff, combined with insecurity and unaffordable medical services, drastically reduced access to primary health-care services. During 1990–2002, about 57 per cent of the population lived on less than US$ 1 a day, and about 74.5 percent lived on less than US$2 a day (UNDP 2004).

The cessation of hostilities and eventual restoration of security countrywide strengthened confidence, which facilitated economic recovery during 2000–2004. A key priority for the Government was to promote efficient, transparent and accountable delivery of services to the poor. In particular, the Government focused on investment in education, health, safe water and sanitation, and housing. With the support and assistance of multilateral and bilateral development partners, strategies were elaborated for improving governance within the public sector, particularly focusing on (i) structural reforms, (ii) decentralization, (iii) financial management and procurement reforms; and (iv) anti-corruption measures.

Source: Government of Sierra Leone (2005)

humanitarian relief, security services, health care, education, water services, etc., should be targeted. Yet in post-conflict countries, communications links are often disrupted, and information systems have not yet become an integral part of reconstruction and development efforts worldwide. Use is sporadic and mostly by international agencies on a piecemeal basis. Thus although ICTs have the potential to enhance post-conflict reconstruction processes, that potential has barely been tapped (Stauffacher, Drake, Currion and Steinberger, 2005).

A review of literature on post-conflict programs in several developing countries indicates limited or no systematic deployment of information systems for public service delivery. A large part of the problem is a lack of existing infrastructure on the ground and the vast sums of money needed to build the necessary telephone lines, cables, satellites, servers and other network components—a huge investment for a post conflict State. However, a primary reason for the limited use of ICTs is insufficient cognizance of their potential dividends.

Awareness is growing, however. At the World Summit on the Information Society, participants adopted a Declaration of Principles that states: "Our challenge is to harness the potential of information and communication technology to promote ... the attainment of a more peaceful, just and prosperous world ... We continue to pay special attention to ... countries recovering from conflict" (WSIS 2003, paragraphs 2 and 16).[17] For post-conflict countries, the corresponding challenge is to take advantage of ICTs and incorporate them into strategies for strengthening public service delivery.

Challenges of providing services in post-conflict situations do not only vary depending on the country and situation. They also vary depending on the specific services themselves. For example in the same country, the challenge of providing education may be different from the challenge of providing judicial services. For example in Rwanda, after the 1994 genocide the country was confronted with an unprecedented number of detainees suspected of having participated in genocide. This was in a situation where the country did not have judges or even courts to handle all the cases. Despite the intervention of the International Tribunal, the challenge remained enormous. The country then had to dig deep in its past traditions to examine how the traditional way of handling cases could be remodeled to handle the situation of post-genocide justice and reconciliation. Thus the birth of the gacaca courts in the country which so far despite some initial disagreements on the system, especially from modern law systems, has provided effective restorative community justice. ◆

2. A multi-stakeholder approach to public service delivery

As stated earlier, in the aftermath of conflict, States rarely have adequate financial, human and other resources to undertake effective reconstruction and rebuilding efforts. In this context, the involvement of multiple stakeholders is necessary. Public officials should adopt an inclusive approach that brings together both State and non-State players, including multilateral and bilateral donors and local and international non-governmental organizations (NGOs), to solidify public service delivery capacities.

Public officials should adopt an inclusive approach that brings together both State and non-State players to solidify public service delivery capacities

However, when foreign donors are involved, there must be an understanding that they are partners in the process, not directors

[17] Source: WSIS declaration of Principles. Document WSIS-03/GENEVA/DOC/4-E. 12 December 2003. p 1-3.
http://www.itu.int/dms_pub/itu-s/md/03/wsis/doc/S03-WSIS-DOC-0004!!MSW-E.doc

Box VI.2 **Health care delivery in Angola: Poor coordination, poor results**

During much of the 20 years of Angola's civil war, health services were provided primarily by the Government in Government-controlled areas. As a result of insecurity in the country, the rural health network went into rapid decline.

With the end of the Cold War and an increased willingness of donors to engage with the Angolan Government, a more varied model of delivery developed that included international non-governmental organizations (INGOs) as providers, with support channeled mainly through the United Nations. However, the Government continued to make only a limited commitment to the provision of health services. With scant strategic direction and minimal outreach to communities, the projects had limited impact, despite donors' efforts to strengthen the Ministry of Health and institutions at the provincial and municipal levels.

When hostilities resumed in 1998, many donors withdrew from Angola, though they continued to fund the INGO programmes there. Many donors and INGOs operated in specific sectors or geographic areas, taking vertical, non-integrated approaches. This led to fragmented service delivery across the country, which was further compounded by humanitarian agencies often working in parallel to Government structures, rather than in concert with them. Throughout this period, less than 30 percent of the total population had access to health care, with care often impossible to get in rural areas.

Source Carlson et al. (2005) ■

of it. Reconstruction and reform programmes must be designed, decided and implemented with the participation and ownership of nationals. Although international attention and large amounts of donor assistance are necessary to end many conflicts, consensus has emerged that State-building interventions will be sustained only through national structures (Brahimi 2007). Thus while donors and development partners can provide assistance and support for the delivery of public services, they must work in tandem with national governments.

It is increasingly being recognized that lack of coordination between and among stakeholders can lead to suboptimal outcomes. When multiple non-integrated programmes are used for service delivery, they often bypass or undermine existing mechanisms, rather than complementing them (Pavenello and Darcy 2008). For example, during the war years in Angola, fragmentation in health service delivery resulted in large part from a lack of coordination among the various players (see box VI.2). By contrast, in Uganda, UNICEF worked closely with the Ministry of Health to provide strong leadership and supervision to the assistance program. Responsibility was eventually turned back to the Ministry, which had developed significant capacity under UNICEF's mentorship. In Afghanistan, the World Health Organization has provided overall coordination, policymaking and strategy support for the health sector (OECD 2008). ◆

3. Strategies for effective delivery of services

Terms such as "recovery", "reconstruction" and "rebuilding" imply a return to the status quo before the conflict. However, since public service delivery might have been inadequate before the conflict, and might even have been a contributing cause, efforts to address service delivery challenges should not necessarily be about restoring pre-conflict economic or institutional arrangements. Rather, the emphasis should be on *"building back differently and better"* (UNDP 2008, p. 5).

Post-conflict situations allow a "window of opportunity" for transformation (UNDP 2007a, p. 1). States can develop better processes and systems aimed at more efficient, effective and inclusive service delivery. The approach needs to be a holistic one, with scaling up of societal, organizational and individual capacities.

In post-conflict situations, the needs relating to public service delivery range from providing humanitarian relief in the short term to ensuring sustainable public service delivery in the long term. In many cases, the ideal mix may be to address both objectives at the same time. In other words, there should be a dual focus on meeting the most pressing needs for security services, clean water, health care, etc., and on building capacity for long-term, equitable, effective provision of services. It is also important to have an integrative approach from the beginning, taking into account the local context and the structures and processes already in place before introducing new initiatives (Pavanello and Darcy 2008).

There should be a dual focus on meeting the most pressing needs for security services, clean water, health care, etc., and on building capacity for long-term, equitable, effective provision of services

Allowing for flexibility and innovation

Post-conflict situations change over time. Therefore, approaches to public service delivery need to be flexible enough to take into account changing realities and development progress. There should also be room for innovation on the ground when difficult circumstances arise. In cases where the State must rely on foreign donors to step in, aid agencies must tailor the delivery of services to the characteristics of the situation and be flexible with respect to entry points and approaches. Service delivery systems should be crafted to use local resources, deliver tangible outputs based on need and target the poorest and most marginalized groups. For example, in Nepal in 1996, the biggest need for public services was in remote, rural communities. Not only were

Post-conflict situations allow a "window of opportunity" for transformation: States can develop better processes and systems aimed at more efficient, effective and inclusive service delivery

113

Box VI.3 **Innovative approaches to service delivery in Nepal**

In February 1996, the Communist Party of Nepal declared a "people's war". The insurgency spread from a limited number of districts in the heartland to all areas of the country. At least 10,000 people, many of them civilians, were killed as a result of the conflict.

Government programmes failed to reach the poorest, especially those who remained in disputed rural areas, leaving many without basic services. Some services—for example, postal and telecommunications—became dysfunctional. Others, such as health and education, continued to function but often under threat, with frontline workers increasingly being intimidated by both the Government security forces and the Communist insurgents who targeted schools, for example, as sites to transmit ideological messages.

In this context, donors formed innovative partnerships with a variety of State and non-State organizations to provide basic public services. For example, Save the Children USA partnered with a local non-governmental organization, BASE, to reintegrate conflict-affected children back into schools. The U.K. Department for International Development (DFID) partnered with government, private sector and civil society stakeholders on the Micro Enterprise Development Programme to support employment and income generation through integrated enterprise development, including community mobilization, market analysis, skills training, technology transfer, product development, micro-credit and marketing linkages. Other partnerships were also formed during this period of conflict.

The approach allowed swift delivery of tangible services directly to communities when the State was not able to perform this function. It had the advantage of meeting demand, as actually voiced by communities, across sectors.

Source: Armon et al.(2004)

these communities difficult to access, but people's freedom of movement was restricted because of security concerns. To successfully provide public services, donors made arrangements on a case-by-case basis with local community organizations and other partners (see box VI.3).

Promoting equality of access and inclusion

Sustaining the peace depends on the capacity of public administration not only to restore service delivery and reconstruct infrastructure, but also to ensure that access to services is equitable. Coverage of all population groups in all geographic areas is important to avoid perceptions of unfairness that could lead to the resumption of conflict. Furthermore, processes and mechanisms being put in place for public service delivery must be designed in an inclusive manner "so that the expectations of a population can be realistically managed and the trust of citizens can be gained" (Brahimi 2007, p. 6).

Ensuring coordination among service providers

In the aftermath of a conflict, various players may rush in to fill the vacuum in delivering assistance. Often, as already noted, they set up parallel structures and systems without adequately coordinating their efforts. Although fragmented approaches may provide urgently needed basic services to far-flung populations in the short term, they are not likely to be sustainable and often lead to wasteful inefficiencies.

Ensuring coordination among various donors, the State and local authorities should be the cornerstone of any service delivery. Effective mechanisms of coordination keep all stakeholders informed and engaged, helping them design assistance programmes that are complementary rather than duplicative. Coordination also allows the sharing of best practices and innovative ideas, creating opportunities to build better and newer approaches to public service delivery. ◆

4. Building ICTs into strategies for citizen-centric public service delivery

Provision of relevant, accurate and timely information is imperative after conflict. In the short term, information about security, food, and services for displaced persons, refugees and devastated communities may literally mean the difference between life and death. In the long run, dissemination of information on various development initiatives, such as public health and education programmes, can contribute to effective service delivery, nation building and sustainable development. Thus the provision of information should be treated as a basic service in post-conflict societies. The tools that can be used for this purpose include radio, television, mobile phones and the Internet. When divorced from politics and used in a neutral fashion, these information and communications technologies can help support the State in reconstruction and rebuilding.

Provision of relevant, accurate and timely information is imperative after conflict. Information about security, food, and services for devastated communities may literally mean the difference between life and death

The role of ICTs in post-conflict situations
In recent times, ICTs have sometimes been used to assist in peacebuilding. For example, during the conflict in the Democratic Repulic of Congo, the United Nations and other donors set up Radio Okapi to help keep peace by disseminating reliable and credible information from an independent source (Putzel and van der Zwan 2005). There is, however, little evidence on the use of information and communications technologies for building public service delivery in the aftermath of conflict. Yet in today's globalized age, the use of ICTs in such situations can be critical. Their ubiquitous 24/7 nature can allow faster sharing and utilization of information, outreach to remote areas, great-

Figure VI.2 **Post-conflict public service delivery and ICT**

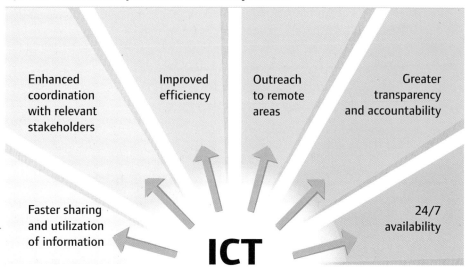

er transparency and better coordination among stakeholders, thereby vastly improving the effectiveness and quality of public service delivery (see figure VI.2).

Service delivery systems should be crafted to use local resources, deliver tangible outputs based on need and target the poorest and most marginalized groups

In the aftermath of conflict, simple technologies such as radio broadcasting may be used to provide security updates, make announcements about service delivery, and share other timely news. More sophisticated information technologies can be useful in mapping service-deficit areas, monitoring service delivery and even building delivery capacity.

In many post-conflict situations, ICTs may be the only way in which governments are able to maintain viable service delivery networks. When infrastructure has been destroyed, mobile telephones can be invaluable for communicating. Geographic information systems (GIS) and remote sensing are helpful in identifying heavily damaged areas and establishing priorities for action. GIS can also ensure uniformity in the distribution of supplies (medicine, food, water, clothing, etc.) to emergency distribution centers" (UNDP 2007b, p. 5).

In Afghanistan, GIS proved useful in rebuilding public telephone booths that had deteriorated during the prolonged conflict. Using a state-of-the-art GIS, local experts mapped the city of Kabul to ascertain where the public booths were located and which were in a state to be repaired. The Ministry of Communications used the information to help refurbish 300 booths in prime locations. This innovative application of GIS mapping eliminated the need for an expensive physical recount and reduced the cost of telecommunications because the city could repair existing telephone booths instead of building new ones (UNDP 2005).

New technologies offer features that may facilitate public service delivery during reconstruction and rebuilding. New technologies include such telecommunication systems as portable satellite earth stations, mobile and portable cellular telephone base stations, and telemedicine video base and remote stations. Emergency telecommunications such as cellular telephones, digital dispatch radios, facsimile, data communications, television and satellites can all complement traditional efforts to secure peace and deliver public services (ITU 2005). For example, the introduction of new technologies to support the provision of water and electricity at the headquarters of the United Nations Interim Force in Lebanon has allowed for constant monitoring of the water supply levels and the electrical grid. The system enables quick repair of any fault before any operations are affected, minimizing service disruptions and engendering cost savings.

New technologies offer features that may facilitate public service delivery during reconstruction and rebuilding

ICTs cut across sectors and provide support to governance processes critical for building public services. The incorporation of ICTs into public sector human resource management strategies can be instrumental in capacity-building and improving the managerial, technical and professional skills of public employees.

ICTs cut across sectors and provide support to governance processes critical for building public services

It is possible to successfully utilize information and communication technologies and frameworks that promote inclusiveness in public service delivery and public sector institution-building after conflict. Horizontal and vertical IT linkages between various public sector institutions and nodal points at the grassroots level in a post-conflict situation can also promote greater participation and social inclusiveness. The information flow can empower public institutions, societal groups and citizens to produce and share information—between and within service delivery sectors—to bring a greater degree of cohesion, transparency and accountability.

ICTs, especially mobile technologies, provide a medium to include the voices of grassroots communities and displaced and marginalized persons. By taking ICTs to the people instead of making the people come to technology hubs, and by creating opportunities for online dissemination of information in far-flung conflict zones, ICTs contribute to more effective service delivery.

ICTs, especially mobile technologies, provide a medium to include the voices of grassroots communities and displaced and marginalized persons

Use of ICTs after disasters: A model for post-conflict situations

ICTs have not yet been widely incorporated into strategies for improving public service delivery in post-conflict situations but have great potential

As mentioned earlier, ICTs have not yet been widely incorporated into strategies for improving public service delivery in post-conflict situations. However, the donor community does have considerable experience using ICTs in disaster relief efforts. Because the challenges in delivering public services after a natural disaster are similar to the challenges in delivering public services after conflict, it is worth reviewing some of the ways that ICTs are being used in post-disaster situations.

Successful initiatives by governments and international organizations include the following:

- The Sahana disaster management system is an open-source Web-based collaboration tool that has facilitated coordination and distribution of relief after natural disasters (see box VI.4). The Sahana project was developed after the Asian tsunami in December 2004 and first used by the Sri Lankan Government; it has since been used by the Governments of the Philippines, Pakistan and Indonesia, as well as by NGOs.

- The United Nations Office for the Coordination of Humanitarian Affairs (OCHA) maintains a website called ReliefWeb, which is the world's leading online gateway to information on humanitarian emergencies and disasters. OCHA also manages the Integrated Regional Information Network (IRIN), an independent news service reporting on humanitarian crises.

- The United Nations World Food Programme (WFP) is an advanced user of ICTs for its field operations. The WFP can rapidly mobilize needed resources in an emergency, thanks to a sophisticated communications network, teams of ICT experts who can be dispatched anywhere in the world on short notice, and a database platform that allows thousands of tons of food supplies to be tracked from procurement to arrival at WFP distribution points (Stauffacher, Drake, Currion and Steinberger 2005).

Some non-governmental organizations are also in the vanguard of using ICTs for disaster relief. They have gone beyond the basic applications of ICTs and are providing interactive tools, searchable databases, maps and GIS and electronic forums for disaster management:

- Aidmatrix is a non-profit that builds partnerships to bring food, clothing, building materials, medical supplies and educational materials to people in need. Using Aidmatrix's Internet

Box VI.4 **Sahana's innovative use of ICTs for humanitarian relief**

Sahana is an integrated set of pluggable, Web-based disaster management applications that provide solutions to large-scale humanitarian problems in the aftermath of a disaster. Its objectives are to:

- Help alleviate human suffering and save lives through the efficient use of ICTs during a disaster;
- Bring together a diverse set of actors—including Government officials, emergency responders, NGOs, spontaneous volunteers and victims themselves—to respond effectively to a disaster;
- Empower the victims, responders and volunteers to help themselves and others;
- Protect victim data and reduce the opportunity for data abuse; and
- Provide a free, open-source solution available to everyone.

Sahana has developed the following open-source software:

- Missing Person Registry, helping to reduce trauma by effectively finding missing persons;
- Organization Registry, coordinating and balancing the efforts of relief organizations in the affected areas and connecting relief groups to help them operate as one;
- Request Management System , registering all incoming requests for support and relief, tracking requests until fulfillment and helping donors match their activities to relief requests;
- Camp Registry, tracking the location and numbers of victims in various camps and temporary shelters set up around the affected area;
- Volunteer Management, coordinating the contact info, skills, assignments and availability of volunteers and responders
- Inventory Management, tracking the location, quantities and expiry of supplies stored for use in a disaster; and
- Situation Awareness, providing a GIS overview of the situation at hand for the benefit of the decision makers.

The system is available for free for anyone to download and customize based on individual requirements.

Source: Sahana website (http://www.sahana.lk/)

platform, donors, NGOs and suppliers are better able to (i) determine which items are needed most where and by whom, (ii) identify available supplies and (iii) coordinate the logistics of their delivery, thereby increasing efficiency when responding to emergencies.

- Télécoms sans Frontières (TSF) builds emergency telecommunications systems in the field to support humanitarian relief operations. TSF has a permanent monitoring center that can deploy specialized teams anywhere in the world in less than 48 hours. Typically, the teams install small but powerful mobile satellite communications to help NGOs and other partners coordinate logistics and related matters.

- MapAction is an NGO that specializes in using satellite earth imaging, data processing and mapping to assist relief missions by supplying up-to-date, real-time maps of disaster areas. MapAction is also part of a consortium called RESPOND that is committed to making geospatial technologies more accessible to the humanitarian-aid community by improving access to maps, satellite imagery and geographic information.

Private and government agencies are also beginning to study how new technologies can be used for conflict prevention

The private sector has also been involved in the field, with one notable example being the Ericsson Response Program, an initiative of the global telecommunications company to assist in relief and reconstruction. Ericsson has been involved in numerous disaster response efforts, from supporting United Nations OCHA with ICT networks in Pakistan following the October 2005 earthquake to bringing teams of Ericsson volunteers and mobile phone systems to the areas struck by the 2004 tsunami in Indonesia and Sri Lanka. Another example is Partners in Technology International (PACTEC), which specializes in the installation of high-frequency radio systems, radio e-mail and satellite telephones in remote environments. PACTEC has undertaken installation projects in Afghanistan, Indonesia (Aceh), Kazakhstan, Mauritania, Morocco, Laos and Senegal and offered technical and business training to local populations to help them develop sustainable business models (Stauffacher et al. 2005).

Although the initiatives described above are part of humanitarian and relief operations, private and government agencies are also beginning to study how new technologies can be used for conflict prevention. At the 2009 Global Media Forum in Bonn, Germany, attended by 1,200 participants from about 100 countries, workshop participants discussed the use of mobile phones as a conflict-prevention tool (Aginam 2009). As time passes, it is to be hoped that stakeholders in post-conflict reconstruction recognize the benefits of using ICTs even more broadly. ◆

5. Lessons learned

- In a post-conflict situation, rapid restoration and rehabilitation of public sector services are imperative to build legitimacy of the State, promote development and prevent a recurrence of conflict.
- To reform citizen-centric public service delivery approaches and practices, governments should work in partnership with non-State actors, including multilateral and bilateral donors, development organizations and civil society organizations. However, any framework aimed at restoring public service delivery must derive its legitimacy from national ownership and local involvement.

- Building effective delivery capacity early on is good governance.
- Public service delivery approaches should allow for flexibility and innovation to meet changing needs and challenging conditions.
- Information and communications technologies can facilitate post-conflict citizen-centric public service delivery and should be increasingly incorporated into the delivery systems and processes used by governments, international organizations, NGOs and private sector groups.
- Contrary to commonly held belief, post-conflict situations not only present challenges, but also numerous opportunities to leapfrog stages of development by adopting innovative practices in public administration, including the application of ICTs in government and service delivery service delivery in the information age we all live in. ■

Bibliography

Chapter I

Alberti, Adriana, ed. (2005). *Human Resources for Effective Public Administration in a Changing World*. New York: United Nations.

Alberti, A. and Jide Balogun, (2005). "Challenges and Perspectives in Reforming Governance Institutions", DPADM Discussion Paper, United Nations.

Brown, Graham, Arnim Langer and Frances Stewart (2008). "A Typology of Post-Conflict Environments: An Overview". CRISE Working Paper 53. Oxford: Centre for Research on Inequality, Human Security and Ethnicity. Available at www.crise.ox.ac.uk/pubs/workingpaper53.pdf

Collier, Paul and Nicholas Sambanis, eds. (2005). *Understanding Civil War*. Washington, DC: World Bank.

Flores, T. E. and Irfan Nooruddin (2007). "Evaluating World Bank Post-Conflict Assistance Programs, 1987–2006". Paper presented at the annual meeting of the International Studies Association 48th Annual Convention, Chicago, Feb. 28. Available at www.allacademic.com/meta/p179938_index.html www.sahana.lk

HIIK (Heidelberg Institute for International Conflict Research) (2007). *Conflict Barometer 2007*. Heidelberg, Germany: Department of Political Science, University of Heidelberg. Available at hiik.de/en/konfliktbarometer/pdf/ConflictBarometer_2007.pdf

Karbo, Tony, and Martha Mutisi (2008). "Psychological Aspects of Post-Conflict Reconstruction: Transforming Mindsets: The Case of the Gacaca in Rwanda". UNDP/BCPR paper prepared for the Ad Hoc Expert Group Meeting on Lessons Learned in Post-Conflict State Capacity: Reconstructing Governance and Public Administration Capacities in Post-Conflict Societies, Accra, Ghana, Oct. 2–4. Available at unpan1.un.org/intradoc/groups/public/documents/UN/UN-PAN032152.pdf

Kauzya, John-Mary (2002). "Approaches, Processes, and Methodologies for Reconstructing Public Administration in Post-conflict Countries". Paper presented at the Fourth Global Forum on Reinventing Government: Capacity Development Workshops, Marrakech, Morocco, Dec. 10–11. Available at unpan1.un.org/intradoc/groups/public/documents/UN/UN-PAN007003.pdf

Schnabel, Albrecht and Hans-Georg Ehrhart, eds. (2006). *Security Sector Reform and Post-Conflict Peacebuilding*. New York: United Nations University Press.

Tschirgi, Neclâ (2004). "Post-conflict Peacebuilding Revisited: Achievements, Limitations, Challenges". Paper presented at the WSP International/IPA Peacebuilding Forum Conference, New York, Oct. 7. Available at www.un.org/esa/peacebuilding/Library/Post_Conflict_Peacebuilding_IPA.pdf

United Nations (1992). "An Agenda for Peace: Preventive Diplomacy, Peacemaking and Peace-keeping". June 17. UN Doc A/47/277 - S/24111. Available at www.un.org/Docs/SG/agpeace.html

―――― (2000) "Report of the Panel on United Nations Peace Operations". Aug. 21. UN Doc A/55/305-S/2000/809. Available at wwwupdate.un.org/peace/reports/peace_operations

―――― (2004a). *A More Secure World: Our Shared Responsibility*. Report of the Secretary-General's High-level Panel on Threats, Challenges and Change. Available at www.un.org/secureworld/report2.pdf

———— (2004b). Executive Summary for *A More Secure World: Our Shared Responsibility*. Report of the Secretary-General's High-level Panel on Threats, Challenges and Change. Available at www.un.org/secureworld/brochure.pdf

———— (2007a). *Building Capacities for Public Service in Post-Conflict Countries*. New York. Available at unpan1.un.org/intradoc/groups/public/documents/UN/UNPAN028646.pdf

———— (2007b). "Governance Strategies for Post Conflict Reconstruction, Sustainable Peace and Development". UN DESA Discussion Paper. Available at unpan1.un.org/intradoc/groups/public/documents/un/unpan028332.pdf

———— (2007c). *The United Nations Development Agenda: Development for All*. New York. Available at www.un.org/en/development/devagenda/UNDA_BW5_Final.pdf

———— UNDP (United Nations Development Programme) (2008). *Post-Conflict Economic Recovery: Enabling Local Ingenuity*. Crisis Prevention and Recovery Report 2008. New York.

———— UNDP (United Nations Development Programme) (2008). *Post-Conflict Economic Recovery: Establishing Enabling Local Ingenuity*. Crisis Prevention and Recovery Report 2008. New York.

———— (2009). *Human Development Report 2008*. New York.

World Bank (2005). *Post-Conflict Reconstruction: The Role of the World Bank*. Washington, DC.

Chapter II

Aiken, Nevin T. (2008). "The Crucial Role of Conflict Transformation in Overcoming the Psycho-Social Challenges to Reconstructing Post-Conflict Governance: A Review and Lessons from Northern Ireland." UNDP/BCPR paper prepared for the Ad Hoc Expert Group Meeting on Lessons Learned in Post-Conflict State Capacity: Reconstructing Governance and Public Administration Capacities in Post-Conflict Societies. Accra, Ghana, Oct. 2–4. Available at unpan1.un.org/intradoc/groups/public/documents/UN/UNPAN032137.pdf

Adamolekun (2005). "On the transferability of governance institutions: two illustrations – Sweden's Ombudsman and Hong Kong's Independent Commission Against Corruption," in G. Bertucci and A. Alberti (eds.), *Methodologies for the transfer of innovations and best practices in governance and public administration*. New York: United Nations.

Balogun, M. Jide, and Mutahaba, Gelase (Eds.) (2002). Economic Restructuring and African Public Administration: Issues, Actions And Future Choices, West Hartford Kumarian Press, pp. 246.

Bar-Tal, Daniel and Gemma H. Bennink (2004). "The Nature of Reconciliation as an Outcome and as a Process". In Yacoov Bar-Siman-Tov, ed., *From Conflict Resolution to Reconciliation*. Oxford: Oxford University Press. Available at tau.ac.il/~daniel/pdf/42.pdf

Brass, Paul R. (1991). *Ethnicity and Nationalism*. New Delhi: Sage.

Brinkerhoff, Derick W. (2007). "Dilemmas and Directions: Capacity Development in Fragile States". *Capacity.org*, issue 32 (Dec.). Available at www.capacity.org/en/journal/feature/dilemmas_and_directions

Connor, Walker (1994). *Ethnonationalism*. Princeton, NJ: Princeton University Press.

Fearon, James D. and David D. Laitin (2000). "Violence and the Social Construction of Ethnic Identity". *International Organization*, vol. 54, issue 4, pp. 845–877.

Garlow, James L. (2002). *The 21 Irrefutable Laws of Leadership Tested by Time: Those Who Followed Them ... and Those Who Didn't*. Nashville, TN: Thomas Nelson Publishers.

Greijn, Heinz (2007). "Rebuilding Liberia". Interview with Dr. Toga McIntosh. *Capacity.org*, issue 32 (Dec.). Available at www.capacity.org/en/journal/interview/rebuilding_liberia

Horowitz, Donald (2000). *Ethnic Groups in Conflict*. Berkeley, CA: University of California Press.

Kaufman, Stuart (2001). *Modern Hatreds: The Symbolic Politics of Ethnic War*. New York: Cornell University Press.

Lake, David A. and Donald Rothchild (1996). "Containing Fear: The Origins and Management of Ethnic Conflict". *International Society*, vol. 21, issue 2, pp. 41–75.

Lakhdar, Brahimi (2007). "State Building in Crisis and Post-Conflict Countries". Paper presented at the 7th Global Forum on Reinventing Government: Building Trust in Government, June 26–29, Vienna, Austria. Available at unpan1.un.org/intradoc/groups/public/documents/UN/UNPAN026305.pdf

Lederach, John Paul (1997). *Building Peace: Sustainable Reconciliation in Divided Societies*. Washington, DC: United States Institute of Peace Press.

Maxwell, John C. (2002). *Leadership 101: What Every Leader Needs to Know*. Nashville, TN: Thomas Nelson Publishers.

M'cleod, H. P. (2007). "The Role of Political Leadership in Post-Conflict Recovery: The Case of Sierra Leone". Paper presented at the 7th Global Forum on Reinventing Government: Building Trust in Government, June 26–29, Vienna, Austria. Available at unpan1.un.org/intradoc/groups/public/documents/un/unpan026844.pdf

Sambanis, Nicholas (2007). "Short and Long-Term Effects of United Nations Peace Operations". *World Bank Economic Review*, vol. 22, issue 1, pp. 9–32.

United Nations (1999). "Governance in Africa: Consolidating the Institutional Foundations". ST/ESA/PAD/SER.E/64. Available at unpan1.un.org/intradoc/groups/public/documents/UN/UNPAN000236.pdf

——— (2007). "Governance Strategies for Post Conflict Reconstruction, Sustainable Peace and Development". DESA Discussion Paper (GPAB/REGOPA cluster), Nov. Available at unpan1.un.org/intradoc/groups/public/documents/un/unpan028332.pdf

Chapter III

Alberti, Adriana (1997). The Role of Public Prosecutors in Democratic Regimes, Ph.D. Thesis Dissertation, European University Institute.

Bergling, Per, Lars Bejstam, Jenny Ederlöv, Erik Wennerström, and Richard Zajac Sannerholm (2008). "Rule of Law in Public Administration: Problems and Ways Ahead in Peace Building and Development." Research Report. Sweden: Folke Bernadotte Academy. Available at www.osce.org/documents/odihr/2009/05/37586_en.pdf

Damaska (1986).

Musa, Shehu A. (2001). "Charter for Public Service in Africa: Strategies for Implementation in Nigeria". Tangier, Morocco: African Training and Research Centre in Administration for Development. Available at unpan1.un.org/intradoc/groups/public/documents/CAFRAD/UNPAN005169.pdf

Ikenberry, G. John (1988). "Conclusion: An Institutional Approach to American Foreign Economic Policy". *International Organization*, vol. 42, issue 1, pp. 219–243.

Jolicoeur, Pierre, ed. (2004). "Études stratégiques et sécurité." Review of *Ending Civil Wars: The Implementation of Peace Agreements*, edited by Stephen John Stedman, Donald Rothchild and Elizabeth M. Cousens. *Études internationals*, vol. 35, issue 2 (June), pp. 379–382. Available at www.erudit.org/revue/ei/2004/v35/n2/009048ar.pdf

Joshi, Janak Raj. (2008). "Making Governance Systems Compatible with the Changing Paradigms of Conflict in Nepal". Draft paper for the Expert Group Meeting on the Reconstruction of Governance and Public Administration after Conflict, Accra, Ghana, Oct. 2–4. Available at unpan1.un.org/intradoc/groups/public/documents/un/unpan032128.pdf

Katorobo, James (2007). "Restoring the Post-Conflict Public Service to Its Position as the Heartbeat of Government". Chap. 4 in *Building Capacities for Public Service in Post-Conflict Countries*, pp. 50–64. New York: UNDESA. Available at unpan1.un.org/intradoc/groups/public/documents/UN/UNPAN028646.pdf

Kauzya, John-Mary. (2005). "Strengthening Local Governance Capacity-Building for Participation" in Dennis Rondinelli and G. Shabbir Cheema (eds.), Reinventing Governemnt for the 21st Century: State capacity in a Globalizing Society, Kumarian Press.

Nakaya, Sumie (2009). "Aid in Post-Conflict (Non) State Building: A Synthesis". New York: City University of New York, Ralph Bunche Institute for International Studies Program on States and

Security. Available at www.statesandsecurity.org/_pdfs/Nakaya.pdf

North, Douglass C. (1990). *Institutions, Institutional Change and Economic Performance: Political Economy of Institutions and Decisions.* Cambridge, U.K.: Cambridge University Press.

Ramsingh, Odette (2008). "The Challenges of Reconstructing the Public Service after Conflict: The Case of the Republic of South Africa". Paper presented to the 2nd Committee of the General Assembly of the United Nations. Nov. 13. Available at esango.un.org/event/documents/Second%20committee%20panel-Ramsinghpaper.doc

United Nations (2001a). Minutes of the session on Governance, Peace and Social Stability at the 3rd United Nations Conference on Least Developed Countries, May 14. Available at www.un.org/events/ldc3/conference/press/devbru4e.htm

——— (2001b). *World Public Sector Report: Globalization and the State.* New York. Available at unpan1.un.org/intradoc/groups/public/documents/UN/UNPAN012761.pdf

——— (2004). "The Rule of Law and Transitional Justice in Conflict and Post-Conflict Societies". Report of the Secretary-General, Aug. 3. UN Doc S/2004/616. Available at daccess-dds-ny.un.org/doc/UNDOC/GEN/N04/395/29/PDF/N0439529.pdf?OpenElement

UNDP (United Nations Development Programme) (1997). "Reconceptualizing Governance". Discussion Paper 2. New York: UNDP Management Development and Governance Division, Bureau for Policy and Programme Support.

Vandemoortele, Jan (2003). "The MDGs and Pro-Poor Policies: Can External Partners Make a Difference?" New York: United Nations Development Programme. Available at www.sarpn.org.za/documents/d0000674/P674-MDGs_pro-poor_policies.pdf

Chapter IV

Barnes, Nathaniel and Bennet Yalartai (2007). "Engaging the Liberian Diaspora: Mobilization of Domestic Resources and Partnership Building for Development: An Alternative Development Model". Available at www.phoenixamericapital.com/files/pdf.pdf

Besteman, Catherine and Lee V. Cassanelli, eds. (2000). *The Struggle for Land in Southern Somalia: The War Behind the War*. London: Haan Associates.

Clarke, Walter and Jeffrey Herbst, eds. (1997). *Learning from Somalia: The Lessons of Armed Humanitarian Intervention*. Boulder, CO, and Oxford: Westview Press.

Dunn, James (1996). *Timor: A People Betrayed*. Sydney: ABC Books.

Finci, Jakob (2007). "Challenges of Reconstituting Conflict-Sensitive Governance Institutions in the Public Service: The Case of Bosnia Herzegovina". Chap. 6 in *Building Capacities for Public Service in Post-Conflict Countries* by the United Nations Department of Economic and Social Affairs, pp. 90–115. New York: United Nations. Available at unpan1.un.org/intradoc/groups/public/documents/UN/UNPAN028646.pdf

Government of Rwanda (1997). "Public Service Reform Programme". Kigali: Ministry of Public Service.

Government of Uganda (1992). "The Public Service Review and Re-organisation Report". Kampala.

Hussein, Ali Dualeh (2002). *Search for a New Somalia Identity*. Nairobi: H. A. Dualeh.

IOM (International Organization for Migration) (2009). *Migration Initiatives Appeal 2009*. Geneva. Available at publications.iom.int/bookstore/free/Migration_Initiatives_09_EN.pdf

Katorobo, James (1996). "Mission Report on Organisational Analysis of the Structure and Functions in the Rwandese Public Service". March. Kigali: Ministry of Public Service.

—— (2003). "Governance and Peace Building in Post-Conflict Countries: The Case of Somalia". Sept. Cameroon: UNDESA.

—— (2007). "Restoring the Post-Conflict Public Service to Its Position as the Heartbeat of Government". Chap. 4 in *Building Capacities for Public Service in Post-Conflict Countries* by the United Nations Department of Economic and Social Affairs, pp. 50–64. New York: United Nations. Available at unpan1.un.org/intradoc/groups/public/documents/UN/UNPAN028646.pdf

Kasozi, A. B. K. (1994). *The Social Origins of Violence in Uganda, 1964–1985*. Kampala: Fountain Publishers.

Kauzya, John-Mary (2000). *Essentials of the Decentralisation Policy of Rwanda*. New York: UNDESA.

—— (2005) Managing Diversity in the Public Service: One of Africa's Least-Tackled Issues: Lessons from South Africa's Experiences" in Sumat Reddy (ed.) Workfroce Diversity. Global Experiences, The ICFAI University Press, India, p. 71-83.

Kyemba, Henry (1997). *The State of Blood*. Kampala: Fountain Publishers.

Langseth, Petter and Justus Mugaju, eds. (1996). *Post-Conflict Uganda: Towards an Effective Civil Service*. Kampala, Uganda: Fountain Publishers.

Lesch, Ann Mosely (1998). *The Sudan: Contested National Identities*. Bloomington and Indianapolis, IN: Indiana University Press.

Levy, Brian and Sahr Kpundeh, eds. (2004). *Building State Capacity in Africa: New Approaches, Emerging Lessons*. Washington, DC: World Bank.

Lewis, I. M. (1993). *Understanding Somalia*. London: Haan Associates.

Mohammed, Osman Omar (1996). *Somalia: A Nation Driven to Despair*. London: Haan Associates.

Mugoju, Justus, ed. (1996) *Uganda's Age of Reforms: A Critical Overview*. Kampala: Fountain Publishers.

NGO QuAM Working Group (2006). "Our Code of Honour: The NGO Quality Assurance Certification Mechanism (QuAM)". Kampala. Available at www.deniva.or.ug/files/quam-downloads_faqs.pdf

Nyaba, P. A. (1997). *The Politics of Liberation in Southern Sudan: An Insider's View*. Kampala: Fountain Publishers.

Okoth, P. Godfrey and Bethwell A. Ogot, eds. (2000). *Conflict in Contemporary Africa*. Nairobi: Jomo Kenyatta Foundation.

Pagaza, I. and D. Argyriades (eds.), *Winning the needed Change: Saving our Planet Earth. A Global Public Service*, OIS, IIAS, 2009.

Pecos, Kutesa (2006). *Uganda's Revolution 1979–1986*. Kampala: Fountain Publishers.

Petterson, Donald (1999). *Inside Sudan: Political Islam, Conflict and Catastrophe*. Boulder, CO, and Oxford: Westview Press.

Pinto, Constancio and Mathew Jardine (1997). *East Timor's Unfinished Struggle*. Boston: South End Press.

Ramsingh, Odette (2008). "The Challenges of Reconstructing the Public Service after Conflict: The Case of the Republic of South Africa". Paper presented to the 2nd Committee of the General Assembly of the United Nations, Nov. 13. Available at esango.un.org/event/documents/Second%20committee%20panel-Ramsinghpaper.doc

SIGMA (Support for Improvement in Governance and Management) (2004). "Public Administration in the Balkans: Overview". Assessment report. Available at www.sigmaweb.org/dataoecd/45/2/34862245.pdf

Tettey, Wisdom J. (2003). "Africa's Options: Return, Retention or Diaspora?" Policy brief. Available at www.scidev.net/en/policy-briefs/africa-s-options-return-retention-or-diaspora-.html

Ulreich, Roland (2001). "Case Study 4, Sierra Leone". Annex 2 of *International Experience with Civil Service Censuses and Civil Service Databases* by Neil McCallum and Vicky Tyler, pp. 80–95. London: International Records Management Trust. Available at www1.worldbank.org/publicsector/civilservice/casestudy4sierraleone.pdf

Chapter V

Blair, Harry (2000). "Participation and Accountability at the Periphery: Democratic Local Governance in Six Countries". *World Development*, vol. 28, issue 1, pp. 21–39.

Bland, Gary (2002). "Decentralization in Guatemala: The Search for Participatory Democracy". *Woodrow Wilson Center Update on the Americas*, issue 3 (March). Available at www.wilsoncenter.org/topics/pubs/DecentGuatemala.pdf

Daskalovski, Zhidas (2007). "Achieving Equal Representation of Ethnic Minorities in Public Administration in the Former Yugoslav Republic of Macedonia". Ch. 14 in *Innovations in Governance in the Middle East, North Africa, and Western Balkans*. New York: United Nations. Available at unpan1.un.org/intradoc/groups/public/documents/UN/UNPAN025283.pdf

Hadi, Suprayoga (2005). "Enhancing Local Governance through Decentralization Policy in Managing

Conflict-Affected Regions in Eastern Indonesia". *Regional Development Dialogue*, vol. 26, issue 2, pp. 96–109.

HPCR (International Association for Humanitarian Policy and Conflict Research) (n.d.). "Uganda: Debates and Challenges in Peacebuilding Initiatives". Case study. Available at www.peacebuildinginitiative.org/index.cfm?pageId=1951

Kauzya, John-Mary (2006). "Decentralization and Decentralized Governance for Enhancing Delivery of Services in Transition Conditions". Background paper for the Regional Forum on Enhancing Trust in Government through Leadership Capacity Building, St. Petersburg, Sept. 28–30.

Kauzya, John-Mary (2005a). "Decentralization: Prospects for Peace, Democracy and Development". DPADM Discussion Paper. New York: UNDESA.

——— (2005b). "Decentralized Governance and Leadership Capacity Building: Symbiotic Linkages and Potential for Local Level Development". Paper for the Ministerial Conference on: Leadership Capacity Building for Decentralized Governance and Poverty Reduction for Sub-Saharan Africa, Kigali, Rwanda, June 6–8.

——— (2007a). "Political Decentralization in Africa: Experiences of Uganda, Rwanda and South Africa". Discussion paper. New York: UNDESA. Available at unpan1.un.org/intradoc/groups/public/documents/UN/UNPAN028411.pdf

——— (2007). In G. Shabbir Cheema and D. Rondinelli (eds.), Decentralizing Governance: Emerging Concepts and Practices, "Political Decentrlilzation in Africa: Experiences of Uganda, rwanda, and South Africa", Brooking Institution Press, Washington D.C. 2007, p. 75-91.

Klot, Jennifer F. (2007). "Women and Peacebuilding". Independent expert paper commissioned by the United Nations Development Fund for Women and the Peacebuilding Support Office.

Available at www.un.org/peace/peacebuilding/Working%20Group%20on%20Lessons%20Learned/WGLLbackgroundpaper%2029.01.08.pdf

Mutabwire, Patrick K. (2008). "Resource Mobilisation for Implementing Decentralisation and Wealth Creation at Local Level: Uganda's Experience". Presentation at a joint meeting of the All Africa Ministerial Conference on Decentralisation and Local Development (AMCOD), and the Conference on Capacity Building on Leadership on Matters of Local Governance and Poverty Reduction in Africa, Yaoundé, Cameroon, May 28–30. Available at unpan1.un.org/intradoc/groups/public/documents/UN/UNPAN030748.pdf

Mutamba, John and Jeanne Izabiliza (2005)."The Role of Women in Reconciliation and Peace Building in Rwanda: Ten Years after Genocide, 1994–2004: Contributions, Challenges, and the Way Forward". Study for the National Unity and Reconciliation Commission, Kigali. Available at www.nurc.gov.rw/documents/researches/Role_of_women_in_peace_building.pdf

Peacebuilding Initiative (n.d.). "Empowerment: Women & Gender Issues: Women, Gender & Peacebuilding Processes". Web page available at www.peacebuildinginitiative.org/index.cfm?pageId=1959#_ftn34

Pereira, Stephen (2003). "Case Study: El Salvador Post-Conflict Program in Democracy and Governance". Report on an RTI International project. Available at www.rti.org/pubs/El_Salvador_Case_Study.pdf

Pottebaum, David and Christopher Lee (2007). "In Control of Their Future: Community-Led Reconciliation and Recovery". Discussion paper. Available at www.dai.com/pdf/POTTEBAUM%20LEE_CommunityLed_Reconciliation_Recovery_16Apr07.pdf

Regional Expert Network on Local Democracy in Asia. (2007). "Summary of E-Discussions: September 1, 2006–Freburary 26, 2007". Bangkok: UNDP. Available at regionalcentrebangkok.undp.or.th/practices/governance/decentralization/documents/RENConsolidatedNote.pdf

Sitoe, Eduardo and Carolina Hunguana (2005). "Decentralisation and Sustainable Peacebuilding in Mozambique: Bringing the Elements Together Again". Research paper written for CEDE. Available at www.nsi-ins.ca/english/pdf/MozambiqueWorkingPaper_Oct_05_Eng.pdf

UNDP (United Nations Development Programme) (2004). "Decentralised Governance for Development: A Combined Practice Note on Decentralisation, Local Governance, and Urban/Rural Development". New York.

———— (2008). *Post-Conflict Economic Recovery: Enabling Local Ingenuity*. Crisis Prevention and Recovery Report. New York.

UNHCR (United Nations High Commission for Refugees) (2008). *Handbook for the Protection of Women and Girls*. Available at www.unhcr.org/protect/PROTECTION/47cfae612.html

United Nations (2005). "2005 World Summit Outcome". UN Doc. A/60/L.1. New York.

(2007). "Governance Strategies for Post Conflict Reconstruction, Sustainable Peace and Development". UNDESA Discussion Paper. Available at unpan1.un.org/intradoc/groups/public/documents/un/unpan028332.pdf

United Nations Peacebuilding Commission (2007a). "Implementing Local Governance and Decentralization Efforts in Post-conflict Contexts". Chair's summary prepared by the Working Group on Lessons Learned for the meeting on Local Governance and Decentralization in Post-War Contexts, New York, Dec. 13. Available at www.un.org/peace/peacebuilding/Working%20Group%20on%20Lessons%20Learned/Decentralization%20and%20Governance%20(13.12.2007)/WGLL%20Chair%20Summary%20_13.12.07_.pdf

———— (2007b). "Local Governance and Decentralization in Postwar Contexts". Background note of the Working Group on Lessons Learned. Prepared for the meeting on Local Governance and Decentralization in Post-War Contexts, New York, Dec. 13. Available at www.un.org/peace/peacebuilding/Working%20Group%20on%20Lessons%20Learned/Decentralization%20and%20Governance%20(13.12.2007)/WGLL%2013.12.07-%20Background%20Note.pdf

United Nations Security Council (2000). Resolution 1325. Women Peace and Security. Available at www.peacewomen.org/un/sc/res1325.pdf

———— (2009). Resolution 1820. Report of the Secretary-General on Peacebuilding in the Immediate Aftermath of Conflict. Available at www.ifuw.org/advocacy/docs/UN_SC_Resolution1820.pdf

Widianingsih, Ida (2006). "Local Governance, Decentralization, and Participatory Planning in Indonesia: Seeking a New Path to a Harmonious Society". In *The Role of Public Administration in Building Harmonious Society: Selected Proceedings from the Annual Conference of the Network of Asia-Pacific Schools and Institutes of Public Administration and Governance (NAPSIPAG)*, edited by Ahmad, Raza. Beijing: Asian Development Bank and NAPSIPAG.

Chapter VI

African Capacity Building Foundation (2008). "Studies in Reconstruction and Capacity Building in Post-Conflict Countries in Africa: Some Lessons of Experience from Mozambique". Revision of 2003 report. Cited in "Comparative Experiences in Developing National Capacities after Conflict: Concept Note" by Peacebuilding Commission Working Group on Lessons Learned.

Aginam, Emeka (2009). "Using Mobile Phone in Conflict Situation Takes Center Stage at Global Media Forum". Online story distributed by AllAfrica Global Media, June 14. Available at allafrica. com/stories/200906171050.html

Armon, Jeremy et al. (2004). "Service Delivery in Difficult Environments: The Case of Nepal". London: U.K. Department for International Development, Asia Policy Division, Nepal Country Office. Available at www.gsdrc.org/docs/open/eb96.pdf

Brahimi, Lakhdar (2007). "State Building in Crisis and Post-Conflict Countries". Paper presented at the 7th Global Forum on Reinventing Government: Building Trust in Government, Vienna, Austria, June 26–29. Available at unpan1.un.org/intradoc/groups/public/documents/UN/UN-PAN026305.pdf

Carlson, Cindy et al. (2005). "Improving the Delivery of Health and Education Services in Difficult Environments: Lessons from Case Studies". London: DFID Health Systems Resource Center. Available at www.dfidhealthrc.org/publications/health_service_delivery/SDDE%20summary_revised%2021feb.pdf

Commins, Stephen (2004). "Service Delivery in LICUS Contexts: Balancing Short-Term Provision with Longer Term Institutional Goals". Discussion note. Available at siteresources.worldbank.org/INTSF/Resources/395669-1126194965141/1635383-1154459301238/LICUSServiceDelivery_ConceptNote.pdf

Dijkzeul, Dennis (2005). *Models for Service Delivery in Conflict-Affected Environments*.London: International Rescue Committee U.K. Available at www.gsdrc.org/docs/open/CON8.pdf

Government of Sierra Leone (2005). "A National Programme for Food Security, Job Creation and

Good Governance (2005 – 2007)". Poverty Reduction Strategy Paper. Available at www.imf. org/external/pubs/ft/scr/2005/cr05191.pdf

Ibrahim Index of African Governance. Available at www. moibrahimfoundation.org/The%20full%20 2008%20Ibrahim%20Index.pdf

ITU (International Telecommunications Union) (2005). *Handbook on Emergency Telecommunications: Part III*. Geneva. Available at www.itu.int/ ITU-D/emergencytelecoms/doc/handbook/ pdf/Emergency_Telecom-e_partIII.pdf

Krug, Etienne G. et al., eds. (2002). *World Report on Violence and Health*. Geneva: World Health Organization.

Organisation for Economic Co-operation and Development (2009). "Service Delivery in Fragile Situations: Key Concepts, Findings and Lessons". *OECD Journal on Development*, vol. 9, issue 3, pp. 9–63. Available at www.oecd.org/dataoecd/17/54/40886707.pdf

Partanen, Mira and Kirsi Joenpolvi, eds. (2007). "Governance Out of a Box: Priorities and Sequencing in Rebuilding Civil Administration in Post-Conflict Countries. Helsinki: Crisis Management Initiative. Available at www.reliefweb.int/rw/ lib.nsf/db900sid/PANA-7D5H2T/$file/ CMI_oct2007.pdf?openelement

Pavanello, Sara and James Darcy (2008). "Improving the Provision of Basic Services for the Poor in Fragile Environments". International Literature Review Synthesis Paper. London: Overseas Development Institute. Available at www.ode.ausaid. gov.au/publications/pdf/synthesis.pdf

Putzel, James and Joost van der Zwan (2005). "Why Templates for Media Development Do Not Work in Crisis States: Defining and Understanding Media Development Strategies in Post-War and Crisis States". London: London School of Economics and Political Science. Available at www.crisisstates.com/download/publicity/crisis_report_low.res.pdf

Stauffacher, Daniel, William Drake, Paul Currion and Julia Steinberger (2005) "Information and Communication Technology for Peace: The Role of ICT in Preventing, Responding to and Recovering from Conflict". New York: United Nations ICT Task Force. Available at www.ict-4peace.org/articles/ict4peace_ebook.pdf

Torres, Magüi Moreno and Michael Anderson (2004). "Fragile States: Defining Difficult Environments for Poverty Reduction". PRDE Working Paper 1. London: U.K. Department for International Development, Policy Division, Reduction in Difficult Environments Team. Available at www.reliefweb.int/rw/lib.nsf/db-900sid/JBRN-7QBDFR/$file/DFID_aug04.pdf?openelement.

UNDP (United Nations Development Programme) (2004). *Human Development Report 2004: Cultural Liberty in Today's Diverse World.* New York.

—— (2005). "Functioning Phones". *UNDP Afghanistan Newsletter*, Aug. 1, p. 1. Available at www.undp.org.af/Publications/Newsletters/english/newsletter_20050801.pdf

—— (2007a). "Capacity Development during Periods of Transition". Practice note. Available at content.undp.org/go/cms-service/download/asset/?asset_id=1635026

—— (2007b). "ICT in Disaster Management". APDIP e-Note 16. Available at www.apdip.net/apdipenote/16.pdf

—— 2008. *Post-Conflict Economic Recovery: Enabling Local Ingenuity.* Crisis Prevention and Recovery Report. New York. Available at www.undp.org/cpr/content/economic_recovery/PCER_rev.pdf

United Nations Peacebuilding Commission (2007). "Implementing Local Governance and Decentralization Efforts in Post-Conflict Contexts". Chair's summary prepared by the Working Group on Lessons Learned for the meeting on Local Governance and Decentralization in Post-War Contexts, New York, Dec. 13. Available at www.un.org/peace/peacebuilding/Working%20Group%20on%20Lessons%20Learned/Decentralization%20and%20Governance%20(13.12.2007)/WGLL%20Chair%20Summary%20_13.12.07_.pdf

World Bank (2009). "Understanding and Responding Effectively to Deterioration in Fragile and Conflict-Affected States". Draft report on April 8 Headline Seminar discussions. Available at siteresources.worldbank.org/EXTLICUS/Resources/511777-1224016350914/Headline_Seminar_Deterioration_Report_FINAL_draft_Apr_8_09.pdf ◆